A GIFT FROM:

_____

TO:

_____

DATE:

_____

God Will Help You

MAX LUCADO
WITH ANDREA LUCADO

THOMAS NELSON
Since 1798

God Will Help You

© 2020 Max Lucado

Text from the following appears in this book: *Anxious for Nothing, You Are Never Alone, Fearless, Jesus,* and *How Happiness Happens.*

Published in Nashville, Tennessee, by Thomas Nelson. Thomas Nelson is a registered trademark of HarperCollins Christian Publishing, Inc.

Thomas Nelson titles may be purchased in bulk for educational, business, fund-raising, or sales promotional use. For information, please email SpecialMarkets@ThomasNelson.com.

Unless otherwise noted, Scripture quotations are from the New King James Version®. © 1982 by Thomas Nelson. Used by permission. All rights reserved. Scripture quotations marked AMPC are from the Amplified® Bible, Classic Edition, copyright © 1954, 1958, 1962, 1964, 1965, 1987 by The Lockman Foundation. Used by permission. (www.Lockman.org). Scripture quotations marked CEV are from the Contemporary English Version. Copyright © 1991, 1992, 1995 by American Bible Society. Used by permission. Scripture quotations marked CSB have been taken from the Christian Standard Bible®, Copyright © 2017 by Holman Bible Publishers. Used by permission. Christian Standard Bible® and CSB® are federally registered trademarks of Holman Bible Publishers. Scripture quotations marked ESV are from the ESV® Bible (The Holy Bible, English Standard Version®), copyright © 2001 by Crossway, a publishing ministry of Good News Publishers. Used by permission. All rights reserved. Scripture quotations marked MSG are from *The Message.* Copyright © by Eugene H. Peterson 1993, 1994, 1995, 1996, 2000, 2001, 2002. Used by permission of NavPress. All rights reserved. Represented by Tyndale House Publishers, a Division of Tyndale House Ministries. Scripture quotations marked NASB are from the New American Standard Bible®. Copyright © 1960, 1962, 1963, 1968, 1971, 1972, 1973, 1975, 1977, 1995 by The Lockman Foundation. Used by permission. Scripture quotations marked NCV are from the New Century Version®. © 2005 by Thomas Nelson. Used by permission. All rights reserved. Scripture quotations marked NIV are from the Holy Bible, New International Version®, NIV®. Copyright © 1973, 1978, 1984, 2011 by Biblica, Inc.®Used by permission of Zondervan. All rights reserved worldwide. www.Zondervan.com. The "NIV" and "New International Version" are trademarks registered in the United States Patent and Trademark Office by Biblica, Inc.® Scripture quotations marked NLT are from the Holy Bible, New Living Translation. © 1996, 2004, 2007, 2013, 2015 by Tyndale House Foundation. Used by permission of Tyndale House Publishers Ministries, Carol Stream, Illinois 60188. All rights reserved. Scripture quotations marked NRSV are from the New Revised Standard Version Bible. Copyright © 1989 National Council of the Churches of Christ in the United States of America. Used by permission. All rights reserved. Scripture quotations marked TLB are from The Living Bible. Copyright © 1971. Used by permission of Tyndale House Publishers a Division of Tyndale House Ministries, Carol Stream, Illinois 60188. All rights reserved.

Any Internet addresses, phone numbers, or company or product information printed in this book are offered as a resource and are not intended in any way to be or to imply an endorsement by Thomas Nelson, nor does Thomas Nelson vouch for the existence, content, or services of these sites, phone numbers, companies, or products beyond the life of this book.

ISBN 978-1-4002-2440-1 (audiobook)
ISBN 978-1-4002-2441-8 (eBook)
ISBN 978-1-4002-2439-5 (HC)

Printed in China

20 21 22 23 24 GRI 10 9 8 7 6 5 4 3 2 1

Contents

Introduction

*H*e's the old guy in the Louisville Cardinal marching band. You can't miss him. Everyone else is college age; he's middle-aged. Everyone else wears a band uniform; he wears a windbreaker and wool cap. Everyone else plays an instrument. Patrick John Hughes pushes a wheelchair. The wheelchair contains his son, Patrick Henry Hughes, a blind, disabled musical genius.

Young Patrick was born on March 10, 1988. The moment he entered the world, good news became bad news. Doctors quickly discovered that his arms and legs wouldn't straighten. And his eyes? He didn't have any.

The older Patrick was shell-shocked. He'd dreamed of raising a son. He planned to turn his backyard into a base-ball field. He envisioned happy hours of running bases, catching pop flies. But now? His son later wrote these words: "On the day I was born, you might say I arrived carrying a bag of lemons . . . I think [my family] would have preferred oranges . . . But you can't turn lemons into oranges, no matter how hard you try. Mom and Dad taught me, you have to hang in there. And once you do, you discover that lemons are pretty cool."[1]

Patrick's parents hung in there, all right.

The father noticed he could calm his infant son by placing him on top of the piano and playing it. The music connected. By nine months, young Patrick was tapping the keys. At the age of two, he was playing requests. In elementary school he played concerts. In high school, he was all-state band and chorus. He graduated with a 3.0 GPA.

By the time he arrived at the University of Louisville, his piano and trumpet skills were well-known. The band director invited him to join the marching band. Wheelchair in a half-time show?

They rigged a special wheelchair with bigger, wider wheels. The teenager and the dad gave it a go at summer band camp: twelve-hour days of ducking tubas and dashing to the right spot without wiping out the entire wind section.

"He hasn't dumped me yet," grinned the boy.

And it appears he never will. Every school day, the father pushed his son to class and sat near him during lectures. He whispered any lessons written on the blackboard. Then, while the rest of the family went to bed, the father left to work the graveyard shift. He would get home at 6 a.m., sleep a few hours, and start it all over again. But this father never complains. "We still say 'why us?'" says the father, "but now it's 'why us? How'd we get so lucky?'"[2]

If their story sounds familiar, it should. That's you and me in the wheelchair, struggling with our limitations. That's you and me in the dark, unable to see a step into the future.

Yet, that force we feel, that guiding hand? God behind us. He shoves, he pulls, he guides, he turns. He can spin us on a dime and has been known to pop a wheelie or two. But he'll never dump us out. Our Father leads us with a sure hand. "Fear not, for I am with you; Be not dismayed, for I am your God. I will strengthen you, Yes, I will help you, I will uphold you with My righteous right hand" (Isaiah 41:10).

Do you have concerns about tomorrow? God doesn't, and he is here to help you.

Are you weary from the struggle? God isn't, and he is here to help you.

Does anxiety steal your sleep? God has comfort and he is here to help you.

No matter the challenge or the question, by God's grace you can face it. He is up to the task. And he will help you.

CHAPTER 1

God Will Help You When You Feel Anxious

*C*hances are you or someone you know seriously struggles with anxiety. According to the National Institute of Mental Health, anxiety disorders are reaching epidemic proportions. In a given year, nearly fifty million Americans will feel the effects of a panic attack, phobias, or other anxiety disorders. Our chests will tighten. We'll feel dizzy and light-headed. We'll fear crowds and avoid people. Anxiety disorders in the United States are the "number one mental health problem among . . . women and are second only to alcohol and drug abuse among men."[1] "The United States is now the most anxious nation in the world."[2] (Congratulations to us!)

The *Journal of the American Medical Association* cited a study that indicates an exponential increase in depression. People of each generation in the twentieth century "were three times more likely to experience depression" than people of the preceding generation.[3]

How can this be? Our cars are safer than ever. We regulate food and water and electricity. Though gangs still prowl our streets, most Americans do not live under the danger of imminent attack. Yet if worry were an Olympic event, we'd win the gold medal! Citizens in other countries ironically enjoy more tranquility. They experience one-fifth the anxiety levels of Americans, despite having fewer of the basic life necessities.[4]

> If worry were an Olympic event, we'd win the gold medal!

Our college kids are feeling it as well. In a study that involved more than two hundred thousand incoming freshmen, "students reported all-time lows in overall mental health and emotional stability."[5] As psychologist Robert Leahy points out, "The average child today exhibits the same level of anxiety as the average psychiatric patient in the 1950s."[6]

We are tense.

Why? What is the cause of our anxiety?

Change, for one thing. Researchers speculate that the Western world's "environment and social order have changed more in the last thirty years than they have in the previous three hundred"![7] Think what has changed. Technology. The existence of the Internet. Increased warnings about global warming, nuclear war, and terrorist attacks.

In addition, we move faster than ever before. Our ancestors traveled as far as a horse or camel could take them during daylight. But us? We jet through time zones as if they were neighborhood streets.

And what about the onslaught of personal challenges? You or someone you know is facing foreclosure, fighting cancer, slugging through a divorce, or battling addiction. You or someone you know is bankrupt, broke, or going out of business.

One would think Christians would be exempt from worry. But we are not. We have been taught that the Christian life is a life of peace, and when we don't have peace, we assume the problem lies within us. Not only do we feel anxious, but we also feel guilty about our anxiety! The result is a downward spiral of worry, guilt, worry, guilt.

It's enough to cause a person to get anxious.

It's enough to make us wonder if the apostle Paul was out of touch with reality when he wrote, "Be anxious for nothing" (Philippians 4:6).

"Be anxious for less" would have been a sufficient challenge. Or "Be anxious only on Thursdays." Or "Be anxious only in seasons of severe affliction." But Paul doesn't seem to offer any leeway here. Be anxious for nothing. Nada. Zilch. Zero. Is this what he meant? Not exactly. He wrote the phrase in the present active tense, which implies an ongoing state. It's the life of perpetual anxiety that Paul wanted to address. The Lucado Revised Translation reads, "Don't let anything in life leave you perpetually breathless and in angst." The presence of anxiety is unavoidable, but the prison of anxiety is optional.

> The presence of anxiety is unavoidable, but the prison of anxiety is optional.

Anxiety is not a sin; it is an emotion. (So don't be anxious about feeling anxious.) Anxiety can, however, lead to sinful behavior. When we numb our fears with six-packs or food binges, when we spew anger like Krakatau, when we peddle our fears to anyone who will buy them, we are sinning. If toxic anxiety leads you to abandon your spouse, neglect your kids, break covenants, or break hearts, take heed. Jesus gave this word: "Be careful, or your hearts will be weighed down with . . . the anxieties of life" (Luke 21:34 NIV). Is your heart weighed down with worry? Look for these signals:

- Are you laughing less than you once did?
- Do you see problems in every promise?
- Would those who know you best describe you as increasingly negative and critical?
- Do you assume that something bad is going to happen?
- Do you dilute and downplay good news with doses of your version of reality?

- Many days would you rather stay in bed than get up?
- Do you magnify the negative and dismiss the positive?
- Given the chance, would you avoid any interaction with humanity for the rest of your life?

If you answered yes to most of these questions, I have a friend for you to meet. Actually, I have a scripture for you to read. I've read the words so often that we have become friends. I'd like to nominate this passage for the Scripture Hall of Fame. The museum wall that contains the framed words of the Twenty-third Psalm, the Lord's Prayer, and John 3:16 should also display Philippians 4:4–8:

> Rejoice in the Lord always. Again I will say, rejoice! Let your gentleness be known to all men. The Lord is at hand. Be anxious for nothing, but in everything by prayer and supplication, with thanksgiving, let your requests be made known to God; and the peace of God, which surpasses all understanding, will guard your hearts and minds through

Christ Jesus. Finally, brethren, whatever things are true, whatever things are noble, whatever things are just, whatever things are pure, whatever things are lovely, whatever things are of good report, if there is any virtue and if there is anything praiseworthy—meditate on these things.

Five verses with four admonitions that lead to one wonderful promise: "the peace of God, which surpasses all understanding, will guard your hearts and minds" (v. 7).

Celebrate God's goodness. "Rejoice in the Lord always" (v. 4). This doesn't mean ignore your circumstances or sugarcoat them. Rejoice in the *Lord.* Celebrate who he is and what he has done in your life, and celebrate his goodness, faithfulness, and forgiveness. These characteristics of God remain true no matter what you are going through.

Ask God for help. "Let your requests be made known to God" (v. 6). Verse five says, "The Lord is at hand." Paul was saying because of the Lord's nearness, we can ask him for what we need. His presence makes way for our prayers.

Leave your concerns with God. "With thanksgiving, let

your requests be made known to God" (v. 6). Don't ignore your concerns. Don't pretend they aren't there. State them, be honest about them, and then leave them in the hands of the Father.

Meditate on good things. "Think about the things that are good and worthy of praise" (v. 8 NCV). Our minds are powerful. They can either be fixated on fear or fixated on good. Which one do you think will ease your anxiety? Paul was tapping into what doctors and therapists would discover centuries later—that we can transform our minds with conscious meditation on the good.

> With God as your helper, you will sleep better tonight and smile more tomorrow.

Celebrate. Ask. Leave. Meditate. C.A.L.M.

Could you use some calm? If so, you aren't alone. The Bible is Kindle's most highlighted book. And Philippians 4:6 is the most highlighted passage.[8] Apparently, we all could use a word of comfort. God is ready to give it.

With God as your helper, you will sleep better tonight and smile more tomorrow. It will require some work on your part. I certainly don't mean to leave the impression that anxiety can be waved away with a simple pep talk. In fact, for some of you, God's healing will include the help of therapy and/or medication. If that is the case, do not for a moment think that you are a second-class citizen of heaven. Ask God to lead you to a qualified therapist who will provide the treatment you need. In the context of scripture, C.A.L.M. is a simple plan and something you can start doing now.

This much is sure: It is not God's will that you lead a life of perpetual anxiety. It is not his will that you face every day with dread and trepidation. He made you for more than a life of breath-stealing angst and mind-splitting worry. He has a new chapter for your life. And he is ready to write it.

Reflection

Spend some time reflecting on what you have read by journaling your thoughts and answers to the following prompts and questions.

1. What is causing you the most anxiety today? Describe the situation and how it's making you feel. What are your thoughts about it? How is it affecting your everyday life?

_____

_____

_____

_____

_____

_____

_____

2. Paul gives four instructions in Philippians 4:4–8. (1) Celebrate God's goodness. (2) Ask God for help. (3) Leave your concerns with God. (4) Meditate on good things. Of those four, which do you practice most often, and which do you do the least? Why do you think this is?

_____

_____

_____

_____

_____

_____

_____

_____

_____

_____

3. Let's walk through the C.A.L.M. method with the scenario you wrote about in the first question.

   Celebrate God's goodness. Spend a few moments writing down the characteristics of God you have seen at work in your life. Describe a time he was faithful to you.

   _____

   _____

   _____

   _____

   _____

   _____

   _____

   _____

Ask God for help. What do you need from him during this time? What would ease your fears and anxiety?

_____

_____

_____

_____

_____

_____

_____

_____

_____

_____

_____

God Will Help You

Leave your concerns with God. List whatever is still on your mind in the space below. Then surrender that list to God by asking him to lift these burdens from you.

_____

_____

_____

_____

_____

_____

_____

_____

_____

_____

Meditate on good things. End your reflection time by meditating on such things as the goodness of God, the beauty of nature, or a piece of art you love—whatever inspires goodness in you. Journal about it in the space below.

_____

_____

_____

_____

_____

_____

_____

_____

_____

God's Word for You

Allow these passages from God's Word to remind you that God will help you if you feel anxious.

> Be anxious for nothing, but in everything by prayer and supplication, with thanksgiving, let your requests be made known to God; and the peace of God, which surpasses all understanding, will guard your hearts and minds through Christ Jesus.
>
> PHILIPPIANS 4:6–8

God's peace is different from temporary or worldly peace. It surpasses understanding.

> "I have told you these things, so that in me you may have peace. In this world you will have trouble. But take heart! I have overcome the world."
>
> JOHN 16:33 NIV

Jesus says, "Take heart." He doesn't say ignore or deny your reality, but rather acknowledge it with the courage we can have in Christ.

> The righteous cry out, and the LORD hears,
> And delivers them out of all their troubles.
> The LORD is near to those who have a broken heart,
> And saves such as have a contrite spirit.
>
> PSALM 34:17–18

The Lord is near when you are brokenhearted. He is not upset with you or disappointed; he is near.

Read the following prayer, silently or aloud. When you have finished praying, spend a moment in silence, listening for the voice of God.

God, I confess to you that I often feel anxious about things I cannot control. Sometimes I doubt your strength and I wonder if you care. I know what your Word says. I can be anxious for nothing and give all my concerns to you, but I need your help to do this. Help me surrender, help me believe, help me know you are good despite my circumstances. Strengthen my faith even when I am anxious. Allow this struggle to deepen our relationship. Thank you for your faithfulness. Remind me of the moments you were faithful in the past so I can cling to them as I walk through difficult seasons of anxiety. In Jesus' name, amen.

CHAPTER 2

God Will Help You Solve Your Problems

*H*ave you ever felt overwhelmed? You know the feeling. You know the paralyzing, deer-in-the-headlights fear that surfaces when the information is too much to learn, the change is too great to make, the decisions are too many to manage, the grief is too deep to survive, the mountain is too tall to climb. Life can easily be overshadowed by one big problem, or many. How to solve it, get out of it, avoid it? We don't know, and so we worry, we fear, we grow preoccupied trying to figure out our solution or our escape plan.

Jesus' disciples felt this way one spring day on a hillside in Galilee.

After these things, Jesus went over to the other side of the Sea of Galilee (also called the Sea of Tiberias), and a huge crowd of people was following him because they had been seeing the signs (the significant things) he was doing with the sick. So Jesus went up into the mountain and was sitting there with his disciples. Now the Passover, the Festival of the Jewish people, was coming up. (John 6:1–4)[1]

For the Jews, Passover was a season of possibilities, a happy recollection of the exodus from Egyptian bondage that whet the appetite for a repeat performance. Would deliverance come in the form of the Nazarene miracle worker? Might he be their Moses and lead them to a promised land? They hoped so. They had seen the signs he had performed. They knew about the healings and the teachings. They followed him around the Sea of Galilee.

> Would deliverance come in the form of the Nazarene miracle worker?

At a certain point Jesus realized that the multitude had nothing to eat. They had no more food in their sacks. They had no food trucks or stores in which to shop. These fifteen thousand-plus people (five thousand men plus women and children) were hungry.

> "Where can we buy enough bread to feed all these people?" (Jesus was asking this to test Philip, because Jesus knew what he himself was going to do.) . . . Philip responded, "Several thousand dollars' worth of bread wouldn't be enough to give even a tiny bite to all these people!" Then one of Jesus' other disciples, Andrew, the brother of Simon Peter, said to Jesus, "There is a boy here with five loaves of barley bread and two fish. Oh, but what are these things when there are all these people?" (vv. 5–9)[2]

Note the thrice-repeated phrase "all these people."

1. Jesus' question: "Where can we buy enough bread to feed *all these people*?" (v. 5)
2. Philip's response: "Several thousand dollars' worth

of bread wouldn't be enough to give even a tiny bite to *all these people!*" (v. 7)

3. Andrew's idea to start with the boy's lunch, but then: "What are these things [loaves and fishes] when there are *all these people?*" (v. 9)

Jesus acknowledged "all these people." Philip saw no help for "all these people." Andrew had an idea, but the suggestion wilted in the face (or faces) of "all these people."

What is your version of "all these people"?

It might be something as pedestrian as "all these diapers" or "all this homework" or "all these long days." Or it might be as disrupting as "all this dialysis," "all this depression," or "all these bills."

Whatever it is, the demand outstrips the supply, and you are left feeling as hopeless as Philip and as meager as Andrew. We'd like to think the followers would respond with more faith. After all, they'd seen water turned into wine and a lame man walk. We'd like to see more spunk, more grit.

More "We can't, but you can, Jesus!" But they and the silent others showed no spark. They counted the hungry people, the money in their bag, and the amount of bread and fish. They did not, however, count on Christ.

And he was standing right there! He could not have been nearer. They could see, hear, touch, maybe even smell him. Yet the idea of soliciting his help did not dawn on them. Even so, Jesus went right to work.

> Jesus said, "Please get the people seated." (There was a lot of grass there.) The people sat down; they numbered about five thousand men. . . . So Jesus took the loaves, and when he had given thanks, he distributed them to those who were seated, and as much fish as they were wanting, too. . . . So when they were satisfied, he said to his disciples, "Please gather up the leftovers so that nothing will be lost." Well, they gathered twelve whole baskets of leftovers from the overflow to those who had eaten the five barley loaves! (John 6:10–13)[3]

The impossible challenge of feeding "all these people" became the unforgettable miracle of all these people fed. What we cannot do, Christ does!

The problems we face are opportunities for Christ to prove this point.

If you see your troubles as nothing more than isolated hassles and hurts, you'll grow bitter and angry. But if you see your troubles as opportunities to trust God and his ability to multiply what you give him, then even the smallest incidents take on significance. Do you face fifteen thousand problems? Before you count your money, bread, or fish, and before you count yourself out, turn and look at the One standing next to you! Count first on Christ.

> The problems we face are opportunities for Christ to prove this point.

He can help you do the impossible. You simply need to give him what you have and watch him work.

"Jesus took the loaves" (v. 11). He didn't have to use

them. He could have turned the nearby bushes into fruit trees. He could have caused the Galilean sea to spew out an abundance of fish. He made manna fall for the Israelites. He could have done it again. Instead, he chose to use the single basket of the small boy.

What's in your basket?

All you have is a wimpy prayer? Give it. All you have is a meager skill? Use it. All you have is an apology? Offer it. All you have is strength for one step? Take it. It's not for you and me to tell Jesus our gift is too small. God can take a small thing and do a big thing. God used the whimper of baby Moses to move the heart of Pharaoh's daughter. He used the faulty memory of an ex-con to deliver Joseph from the prison and send him to the palace. He used David's sling and stone to overthrow the mighty Goliath. He used three nails and a crude cross to redeem humanity.[4] If God can turn a basket into a buffet with food to spare, don't you think he can do something with your five loaves and two fishes of faith?

When we are in the midst of the problem, it's difficult to

see a way out. When we have limited resources, it's difficult to imagine being able to work with what we have. But God is above time. He sees the end. He already knows how he will solve your problem. And God has infinite resources. He isn't limited by finances, a packed calendar, or a difficult boss. He is the one who makes a way when there seems to be no way. You don't have to solve this yourself, and God doesn't expect you to. You are the human. He is the divine being. Let him intervene.

The next time you feel overwhelmed, remind yourself of the One who is standing next to you. You aren't alone. You aren't without help. What bewilders you does not bewilder him. Your uphill is downhill for him. He is not stumped by your problem. When you present your needs to him, he never, ever turns to the angels and says, "Well, it finally happened. I've been handed a code I cannot crack. The demand is too great, even for me."

You may feel outnumbered, but he does not. Give him what you have, offer thanks, and watch him go to work.

Reflection

Spend some time reflecting on what you have read by journaling your thoughts and answers to the following prompts and questions.

1. What problem are you facing right now?

_____

_____

_____

What resources do you have to help fix this problem?

_____

_____

_____

_____

What resources are you lacking?

_____

_____

_____

_____

_____

2. Have you asked God to help you with this problem? Why or why not?

_____

_____

_____

_____

_____

_____

3. Read John 6:1–13 again. Underline everything Jesus did and said in this passage. Of those things you underlined, what stands out to you most and why?

_____

_____

_____

_____

_____

4. If Jesus were sitting with you right now, how would you tell him about your problem? How would you ask him for what you need?

_____

_____

_____

_____

5. Make a list of what you need to solve your problem.

_____

_____

_____

_____

_____

_____

Do you believe God can provide these things for you? Why or why not?

_____

_____

_____

_____

_____

God's Word for You

Allow these passages from God's Word to remind you that God will help you solve your problems.

> Trust in the LORD with all your heart,
> And lean not on your own understanding;
> In all your ways acknowledge Him,
> And He shall direct your paths.

PROVERBS 3:5–6

You may not know which way to go, but the Lord does. Let him lead you.

> But those who wait on the LORD
> Shall renew their strength;
> They shall mount up with wings like eagles,
> They shall run and not be weary,
> They shall walk and not faint.

ISAIAH 40:31

Waiting can feel impossible, but it can also bring renewal and strength.

Now to Him who is able to do exceedingly abundantly above all that we ask or think, according to the power that works in us, to Him be glory in the church by Christ Jesus to all generations, forever and ever. Amen.

EPHESIANS 3:20–21

God is not limited to doing exactly what we ask, or just a little less, or even a little more. He is able to do exceedingly abundantly above all that we ask!

"What man is there among you who, if his son asks for bread, will give him a stone? Or if he asks for a fish, will he give him a serpent? If you then, being evil, know how to give good gifts to your children, how much more will your Father who is in heaven give good things to those who ask Him!"

MATTHEW 7:9–11

In the same way you would not deprive your child of basic food and drink, your Father will not deprive you of what you need.

Read the following prayer, silently or aloud. When you have finished praying, spend a moment in silence, listening for the voice of God.

God, I praise you for who you are and who you have proven yourself to be in my life. You are faithful, good, and true. You care about your children. You care about the details of our lives. You are not distant. You are near. Be near to me today in the midst of the problems I am facing. I don't know how to solve them myself. I don't have enough money, time, or patience, and I don't know what to do. Give me what I need for each moment. My daily bread. Provide for me in ways I didn't think were possible. I don't have much to give except an open heart, my trust in you, and hope. I ask now that you would do immeasurably more than I could ever ask or imagine. Thank you for getting me through this day and the ones to come. In Jesus' name, amen.

CHAPTER 3

God Will Help You Through Your Fears

*A*s famous lakes go, Galilee—only thirteen miles at its longest, seven and a half at its widest—is a small, moody one. The diminutive size makes it more vulnerable to the winds that howl out of the Golan Heights. They turn the lake into a blender, shifting suddenly, blowing first from one direction, then another. Winter months bring such storms every two weeks or so, churning the waters for two to three days at a time.[1]

When Peter and a few other disciples found themselves in the middle of Galilee one stormy night, they knew they were in trouble: "But the boat was now in the middle of the sea, tossed by the waves, for the wind was contrary" (Matthew 14:24).

What should have been a sixty-minute cruise became a nightlong battle. The boat lurched and lunged like a kite in a

March wind. Sunlight was a distant memory. Rain fell from the night sky in buckets. Lightning sliced the blackness with a silver sword. Winds whipped the sails, leaving the disciples "in the middle of the sea, tossed by the waves." Apt description, perhaps, for your stage in life? Perhaps all we need to do is substitute a couple of nouns . . .

In the middle of a divorce, tossed about by guilt.

In the middle of debt, tossed about by creditors.

In the middle of a recession, tossed about by stimulus packages and bailouts.

The disciples fought the storm for nine cold, skin-drenching hours. And about 4:00 a.m. the unspeakable happened. They spotted someone coming on the water. "'A ghost!' they said, crying out in terror" (v. 26 MSG).

They didn't expect Jesus to come to them this way.

Neither do we. We expect him to come in the form of peaceful hymns or Easter Sundays or quiet retreats. We expect to find Jesus in morning devotionals, church suppers, and meditation. We never expect to see him in a bear market, pink slip, lawsuit, foreclosure, or war. We never expect to see him in a storm. But it is in storms that he does his finest work, for it is in storms that he has our keenest attention.

Jesus replied to the disciples' fear with an invitation worthy of inscription on every church cornerstone and residential archway. "'Don't be afraid,' he said. 'Take courage. I am here!'" (v. 27 NLT).

> We never expect to see Jesus in a storm.

Power inhabits those words. To awaken in an ICU and hear your husband say, "I am here." To lose your retirement yet feel the support of your family in the words "We are here." When a Little Leaguer spots Mom and Dad in the bleachers watching the game, "I am here" changes everything. Perhaps that's why God repeats the "I am here" pledge so often.

The Lord is near (Philippians 4:5 NIV).
You are in me, and I am in you (John 14:20 NIV).
I am with you always, to the very end of the age (Matthew 28:20 NIV).

43

I give them eternal life, and they shall never perish;
no one will snatch them out of my hand (John
10:28 NIV).

Nothing can ever separate us from God's love.
Neither death nor life, neither angels nor demons,
neither our fears for today nor our worries about
tomorrow—not even the powers of hell can
separate us from God's love (Romans 8:38 NLT).

We cannot go where God is not. Look over your shoulder; that's God following you. Look into the storm; that's Christ coming toward you.

Much to Peter's credit, he took Jesus at his word. "'Lord, if it is You, command me to come to You on the water.' So He said, 'Come.' And when Peter had come down out of the boat, he walked on the water to go to Jesus" (Matthew 14:28–29).

Peter never would have made this request on a calm sea. Had Christ strolled across a lake that was as smooth as mica, Peter would have applauded, but I doubt he would have stepped out of the boat. Storms prompt us to take unprecedented journeys. For a few historic steps and heart-stilling moments, Peter did the impossible. He defied every law of gravity and nature; "he walked on the water to go to Jesus."

My editors wouldn't have tolerated such brevity. They would have flooded the margin with red ink: "Elaborate! How quickly did Peter exit the boat? What were the other disciples doing? What was the expression on his face? Did he step on any fish?"

Matthew had no time for such questions. He moves us quickly to the major message of the event: where to stare in a storm. "But when [Peter] saw that the wind was boisterous, he was afraid; and beginning to sink he cried out, saying, 'Lord, save me!'" (v. 30).

> Storms prompt us to take unprecedented journeys.

A wall of water eclipsed his view. A wind gust snapped the mast with a crack and a slap. A flash of lightning illuminated the lake and the watery Appalachians it had become. Peter shifted his attention away from Jesus and toward the squall, and when he did, he sank like a brick in a pond. Give the storm waters more attention than the Storm Walker and get ready to do the same.

Whether or not storms come, we cannot choose. But where we stare during a storm, that we can. I found a direct example of this truth while sitting in my cardiologist's office. My heart rate was misbehaving, taking the pace of a NASCAR race and the rhythm of a Morse code message. So I went to a specialist. After reviewing my tests and asking me some questions, the doctor nodded knowingly and told me to wait for him in his office.

I didn't like being sent to the principal's office as a kid. I don't like being sent to the doctor's office as a patient. But I went in, took a seat, and quickly noticed the doctor's abundant harvest of diplomas. They were everywhere, from everywhere. One degree from the university. Another degree from a residency.

The more I looked at his accomplishments, the better I felt. *I'm in good hands.* About the time I leaned back in the chair to relax, his nurse entered and handed me a sheet of paper. "The doctor will be in shortly," she explained. "In the meantime he wants you to acquaint yourself with this information. It summarizes your heart condition."

I lowered my gaze from the diplomas to the summary of the disorder. As I read, contrary winds began to blow. Unwelcome words like *atrial fibrillation*, *arrhythmia*, *embolic stroke*, and *blood clot* caused me to sink into my own Sea of Galilee.

What happened to my peace? I was feeling much better a moment ago. So I changed strategies. I counteracted diagnosis with diplomas. In between paragraphs of bad news, I looked at the wall for reminders of good news. That's what God wants us to do.

His call to courage is not a call to naïveté or ignorance. We aren't to be oblivious to the overwhelming challenges that life brings. We're to counterbalance them with long looks at God's accomplishments. "We must pay much closer attention to what we have heard, so that we do not drift away from it" (Hebrews 2:1 NASB). Do whatever it takes to keep your gaze on Jesus.

This is what Peter learned to do. After a few moments of flailing in the water, he turned back to Christ and cried, "'Lord, save me!' Immediately Jesus reached out his hand and caught him. 'You of little faith,' he said, 'why did you doubt?' And when they climbed into the boat, the wind died down" (Matthew 14:30–32 NIV).

> Do whatever it takes to keep your gaze on Jesus.

Jesus could have stilled this storm hours earlier. But he didn't. He wanted to teach the followers a lesson. Jesus could have calmed your storm long ago too. But he hasn't. Does he also want to teach you a lesson? Could that lesson read something like this: "Storms are not an option, but fear is"?

God has hung his diplomas in the universe. Rainbows, sunsets, horizons, and star-sequined skies. He has recorded his accomplishments in Scripture. We're not talking six thousand hours of flight time. His résumé includes Red Sea openings. Lions' mouths closings. Goliath topplings. Lazarus raisings. Storm stillings and strollings.

His lesson is clear. He's the commander of every storm. Are you scared in yours? Then stare at him.

Reflection

Spend some time reflecting on what you have read by journaling your thoughts and answers to the following prompts and questions.

1. Where do you typically fix your gaze during a stormy time in life? On God, on others, on a coping mechanism? Why do those things draw your gaze?

   _____

   _____

   _____

   _____

   _____

2. Spend some time imagining what it would have been like to be a disciple in this story, on a boat in the middle of the Sea of Galilee during a storm. How would you feel? What kind of thoughts would you have been thinking?

_____

_____

_____

_____

Now, imagine what it would be like to see Jesus suddenly appear in the midst of your fear and uncertainty on the boat. How would your thoughts and feelings change?

_____

_____

_____

3. Think of a storm you are going through now. What are your fears in the midst of it? List them below.

_____

_____

_____

_____

What "diplomas" does God have that would allow him to ease these fears (for example, strength, forgiveness, or love)?

_____

_____

_____

_____

_____

God's Word for You

Allow these passages from God's Word to remind you that God will help you through your fears.

> "Have I not commanded you? Be strong and courageous.
> Do not be afraid; do not be discouraged, for the LORD
> your God will be with you wherever you go."
>
> JOSHUA 1:9 NIV

The Lord doesn't just take away our fear; he replaces it with strength and courage.

> But now, thus says the LORD, who created you, O
> Jacob,
> And He who formed you, O Israel:
> "Fear not, for I have redeemed you;
> I have called you by your name;
> You are Mine.
> When you pass through the waters, I will be with you;

And through the rivers, they shall not overflow you.
When you walk through the fire, you shall not be
      burned,
Nor shall the flame scorch you.
For I am the LORD your God."

ISAIAH 43:1–3

The Lord has called you by name and you are his. Allow this truth to comfort your fears.

"Peace I leave with you, My peace I give to you; not as the world gives do I give to you. Let not your heart be troubled, neither let it be afraid."

JOHN 14:27

These are the words of Christ. Receive his peace as a gift that has already been offered to you.

"There is no fear in love; but perfect love casts out fear."

1 JOHN 4:18

Your fear is not of God or from God. His love casts out fear.

Read the following prayer, silently or aloud. When you have finished praying, spend a moment in silence, listening for the voice of God.

God, thank you for reminding me of your power today. Just as Jesus walked on water, so can you calm the storms around me. I often feel afraid when life gets stormy. I can't see my way out. I feel vulnerable to what I cannot control. Help me fix my gaze on you today. Remind me of who you are and what you are capable of. Ease my fears and replace them with peace. Calm my anxious thoughts. Help me love those around me and be present with them, which is hard to do during a difficult time. Whenever I feel afraid, or my thoughts feel out of control, may I see the image of Christ walking on the water extending his hand to help me. May I trust Christ more than myself, more than others, more than what I tend to focus on during times like this. May my gaze always be fixed on him. In Jesus' name I pray, amen.

CHAPTER 4

God Will Help You When You Feel Stuck

*H*ave you ever felt stuck? Lodged between a rock and a hard place, unable to escape? Mired in the mud of resentment, bogged down in debt, trapped in a dead-end career, up to your waist in the swamp of an unsolvable conflict? Stuck? Stuck with parents who won't listen or employees who won't change? Stuck with a harsh boss or a stubborn addiction?

Stuck.

The man near the pool of Bethesda didn't use the word *stuck*, but he could have. For thirty-eight years near the edge of a pool, it was just him, his mat, and his paralyzed body. And since no one would help him, help never came.

He was seriously, unquestionably, undeniably stuck.

Afterward Jesus returned to Jerusalem for one of the Jewish holy days. Inside the city, near the Sheep Gate, was the pool of Bethesda, with five covered porches. Crowds of sick people—blind, lame, or paralyzed—lay on the porches. One of the men lying there had been sick for thirty-eight years. (John 5:1–5 NLT)

They must have made a miserable sight: crowds of people—blind, lame, despondent, dejected, one after the other—awaiting their chance to be placed in the pool where healing waters bubbled up.[1]

The pool was large: 393 feet long, 164 feet wide, and 49 feet deep.[2] Five porticos were built to shelter the infirm from the sun. Like wounded soldiers on a battlefield, the frail and feeble collected near the pool.

We see such sights still today. The underfed refugees at the camps in Syria. The untreated sick on the streets of Bangladesh. The unnoticed orphans of China. Unattended indigents, unwelcomed immigrants—they still gather. In Central Park. At Metropolitan Hospital. In Joe's Bar and Grill. It's any collection of huddled masses characterized by pain and suffering.

Can you envision them?

And, more important, can you envision Jesus walking among them?

All the gospels' stories of help and healing invite us to embrace the wonderful promise: "Wherever [Jesus] went he healed people of every sort of illness. And what pity he felt for the crowds that came, because their problems were so great and they didn't know what to do or where to go for help" (Matthew 9:35–36 TLB).

Jesus was drawn to the hurting, and on that particular day he was drawn to the pool of Bethesda. What emotions did he feel as he surveyed the mass of misfortune? What thoughts did he have as he heard their appeals? Did they touch his robe as he walked past? Did he look into their faces? It was a sad, piteous sight. Yet Jesus walked into the midst of it.

His eyes landed on the main character of this miracle, a man who "had been sick for thirty-eight years. When Jesus saw him and knew he had been ill for a long time, he asked him, 'Would you like to get well?' 'I can't, sir,' the sick man said, 'for I have no one to put me into the pool when the water bubbles up. Someone else always gets there ahead of me'" (John 5:5–7 NLT).

What an odd question to ask a sick person: Would you like to get well?

I've been visiting the sick since 1977. My first ministry assignment was a pastoral internship program that included regular rounds at hospitals in St. Louis, Missouri. Since that day I've spoken with hundreds, maybe thousands, of sick people: in churches, hospitals, eldercare homes, and hospice care units. I've prayed for migraines and measles. I've anointed with oil, held the hands of the dying, whispered prayers, raised my voice, knelt at bedsides, read Scripture, and stood with worried families. But I have never ever—not once—asked the infirmed, "Would you like to get well?"

> "Would you like to get well?"

Why would Jesus pose such a question? Our only clue is the phrase "When Jesus saw him and knew he had been ill for a long time" (v. 6 NLT). The man was two years shy of four decades as an invalid. Thirty-eight years—almost the amount of time the Hebrews wandered in the desert. It was the duration of the condition that prompted Christ to ask, "Would you like to get well?"

What tone did Jesus use? Was he the compassionate shepherd? Did he ask the question with trembling voice and softness? Maybe. But I don't think so. The phrase "when Jesus . . . knew he had been ill for a long time" makes me think otherwise. And the response of the man convinces me.

> "I can't, sir," the sick man said, "for I have no one to put me into the pool when the water bubbles up. Someone else always gets there ahead of me." (v. 7 NLT)

Really? No one will help you? Someone else always gets ahead of you? In thirty-eight years you couldn't inch your way down to the pool? Persuade someone to give you a hand? Thirty-eight years and absolutely no progress?

In that context Christ's question takes on a firm tone: Do you want to get well? Or do you like being sick? You have a good thing going here. Your tin cup collects enough coins to buy the beans and bacon. Not a bad gig. Besides, healing would be disruptive. Getting well means getting up, getting a job, and getting to work. Getting on with life. Do you really want to be healed?

That's the question Christ asked then. That's the question Christ asks all of us.

Do you want to get . . . sober? Solvent? Educated? Better? Do you want to get in shape? Over your past? Beyond your upbringing? Do you want to get stronger, healthier, happier? Would you like to leave Bethesda in the rearview mirror? Are you ready for a new day, a new way? Are you ready to get unstuck?

Ah, there it is. There's the word. That's the descriptor.

Unstuck.

Dislodged.

Pried loose.

> Getting well means getting up, getting a job, and getting to work.

Set free.

Let go.

Unshackled.

Unstuck.

Life feels stuck when life makes no progress. When you battle the same discouragement you faced a decade ago or struggle with the same fears you faced a year ago. When you wake up to the same hang-ups and habits. When Bethesda becomes a permanent mailing address. When you feel as though everyone gets to the pool before you and nobody wants to help you.

If that is you, then pay attention to the promise of this miracle. Jesus sees you. This Bethesda of your life? Others avoid you because of it. Jesus walks toward you in the midst of it. He has a new version of you waiting to happen. He says to you what he said to the man: "Stand up, pick up your mat, and walk!" (v. 8 NLT).

Stand up. Do something. Take action. Write a letter. Apply for the job. Reach out to a counselor. Get help. Get radical. Stand up.

Pick up your mat. Make a clean break with the past. Clean out your liquor cabinet. Throw out the junky novels. Quit hanging with the bad crowd. Drop the boyfriend like a bad habit. Put porn filters on your phone and computer. Talk to a debt counselor.

And walk. Lace up your boots and hit the trail. Assume that something good is going to happen. Set your sights on a new destination, and begin the hike. Getting unstuck means getting excited about getting out.

Heed the invitation of this miracle: believe in the Jesus who believes in you. He believes that you can rise up, take up, and move on. You are stronger than you think. "'I know the plans I have for you,' declares the LORD, 'plans to prosper you and not to harm you, plans to give you hope and a future'" (Jeremiah 29:11 NIV).

> Believe in the Jesus who believes in you.

What will God do for you? I cannot say. Those who claim they can predict the miracle are less than honest. God's help, while ever present, is ever specific. It is not ours to say what God will do. Our job is to believe he will do something. It simply falls to us to stand up, take up, and walk.

Jesus is serious about this command. When he found the just-healed man in the temple, he told him, "See, you have been made well. Sin no more, lest a worse thing come upon you" (John 5:14). To indulge in inertia is to sin! Stagnant, do-nothingness is deemed as a serious offense.

No more Bethesda for you. No more waking up and going to sleep in the same mess. God dismantled the neutral gear from your transmission. He is the God of forward motion, the God of tomorrow. He is ready to write a new chapter in your biography.

The man in John's story had waited thirty-eight years, but, God bless him, he wasn't about to wait another day. He could have. To be honest, I thought he would have. Listening to his excuse, I would have thought he'd stay stuck forever. But something about the presence of Christ, the question of Christ, and the command of Christ convinced him not to wait another day.

Let's join him. Ask the Lord this question: What can I

do today that will take me in the direction of a better tomorrow? Keep asking until you hear an answer. And once you hear it, do it. Stand up, take up, and walk.

Reflection

Spend some time reflecting on what you have read by journaling your thoughts and answers to the following prompts and questions.

1. Write down any thoughts you have on the story of the man by the pool of Bethesda. Do you have any tension with the text? Questions? Any inspiration or conviction?

_____

_____

_____

2. In what area of your life do you feel stuck right now and why? How long have you felt stuck there?

_____

_____

_____

_____

_____

Answer the question Jesus asked the man by the pool of Bethesda: "Do you want to get well?" Why or why not?

_____

_____

_____

_____

_____

God's Word for You

Allow these passages from God's Word to remind you that God will help you if you are stuck.

> "Do not remember the former things,
> Nor consider the things of old.
> Behold, I will do a new thing,
> Now it shall spring forth;
> Shall you not know it?
> I will even make a road in the wilderness
> And rivers in the desert."
>
> ISAIAH 43:18–19

The imagination of God is great, much greater than ours. He can create new from old.

Let us lay aside every weight, and the sin which so easily ensnares us, and let us run with endurance the race that is set before us, looking unto Jesus, the author and finisher of our faith, who for the joy that was set before Him endured the cross, despising the shame, and has sat down at the right hand of the throne of God.

HEBREWS 12:1–2

Sometimes getting unstuck requires action on our part. Lay aside the weight of sin, and run!

"Ask, and it will be given to you; seek, and you will find; knock, and it will be opened to you. For everyone who asks receives, and he who seeks finds, and to him who knocks it will be opened."

MATTHEW 7:7–8

Do you want to get well? Just ask God.

Read the following prayer, silently or aloud. When you have finished praying, spend a moment in silence, listening for the voice of God.

Father, thank you for giving us your Word to protect us, convict us, and teach us. I confess I have been like the man by the pool of Bethesda. I have not wanted to be healed. I have wanted to remain stuck because I am afraid of what healing will look like and what that will mean not only for me but for my family and my friends. Forgive me for refusing healing, and soften my heart to receive it. Ultimately, I don't want to remain stuck forever, but I need help getting out. Give me the strength to ask for help and to take the necessary steps toward freedom. Help me trust you with the process. Surround me with a safe and loving community as I walk through this journey. Thank you for caring about me and thank you most of all for saving me. Through your Son, Jesus Christ, I pray, amen.

CHAPTER 5

God Will Help You When You Feel Lonely

I am watching a family of black-tailed squirrels. I should be working on a sermon but can't focus. They seem set on entertaining me. They scamper amid the roots of the tree north of my office. We've been neighbors for three years now. They watch me peck at the keyboard. I watch them store their nuts and climb the trunk. We're mutually amused. I could watch them all day. Sometimes I do.

But I've never considered becoming one of them. The squirrel world holds no appeal to me. Who wants to sleep next to a hairy rodent with beady eyes? (No comments from my wife, Denalyn, please.) Give up the Rocky Mountains, bass fishing, weddings, and laughter for a hole in the ground and a diet of dirty nuts? Count me out.

But count Jesus in. What a world he left. Our classiest mansion would be a tree trunk to him. Earth's finest cuisine would be walnuts on heaven's table. And the idea of becoming a squirrel with claws and tiny teeth and a furry tail? It's nothing compared to God's becoming an embryo and entering the womb of Mary.

Nonetheless, he did. The God of the universe was born into the poverty of a peasant and spent his first night in the feed trough of a cow. "The Word became flesh and lived among us" (John 1:14 NRSV). The God of the universe left the glory of heaven and moved into the neighborhood. Our neighborhood! Who could have imagined he would do such a thing?

> The God of the universe left the glory of heaven and moved into the neighborhood.

When God came to earth, he ensured our salvation, he ensured grace, he ensured hope, and he ensured something else—that we would never be lonely again.

Perhaps you feel lonely today. Perhaps you've felt lonely for weeks or even months. We cannot avoid loneliness. It is common to every human experience. You're the new person in town, or your best friend moves away, or for whatever reason community is hard to find right now. But in Christ, God is always near. He loves to be with the ones he loves, so much so that the One who made everything "made himself nothing" (Philippians 2:7 NCV). Christ made himself small. He made himself dependent on lungs, a larynx, and legs. He experienced hunger and thirst. He went through all the normal stages of human development. He was taught to walk, stand, wash his face, and dress himself. His muscles grew stronger; his hair grew longer. His voice cracked when he passed through puberty. He was genuinely human.

When he was "full of joy" (Luke 10:21 NIV), his joy was authentic. When he wept for Jerusalem (Luke 19:41), his tears were as real as yours or mine. When he asked, "How long must I put up with you?" (Matthew 17:17 NLT), his frustration was honest. When he cried out from the cross, "My God, My God, why have You forsaken Me?" (Matthew 27:46), he needed an answer.

He took "the very nature of a servant" (Philippians 2:7 NIV). He became like us so he could serve us! He entered the world not to demand our allegiance but to display his affection.

Jesus may have had pimples. He may have been tone deaf. Perhaps a girl down the street had a crush on him or vice versa. It could be that his knees were bony. One thing's for sure: he was, while completely divine, completely human.

Why? Why did Jesus expose himself to human difficulties? Growing weary in Samaria (John 4:6). Disturbed in Nazareth (Mark 6:6). Angry in the temple (John 2:15). Sleepy in the boat on the Sea of Galilee (Mark 4:38). Sad at the tomb of Lazarus (John 11:35). Hungry in the wilderness (Matthew 4:2).

Why did he endure all these feelings? Because he knew you would feel them too. He knew you would be weary, disturbed, lonely, and angry.

He knew you'd be sleepy, grief stricken, and hungry. He knew you'd face pain. If not the pain of the body, the pain of the soul . . . pain too sharp for any drug. He knew you'd face thirst. If not a thirst for water, at least a thirst for truth, and the truth we glean from the image of a thirsty Christ is that he understands.

When we feel lonely, knowing someone understands

us can make all the difference. You can be surrounded by people but still feel lonely if you don't feel known. And, you can be alone but not feel lonely when you are known. God became flesh so we would always feel known by him. Consider some of the qualities of Jesus:

Born to a mother.
Acquainted with physical pain.
Enjoys a good party.
Rejected by friends.
Unfairly accused.
Loves stories.
Reluctantly pays taxes.
Sings.
Turned off by greedy religion.
Feels sorry for the lonely.
Unappreciated by siblings.
Stands up for the underdog.
Kept awake at night by concerns.
Known to doze off in the midst of trips.

Accused of being too rowdy.
Afraid of death.

I could be describing Jesus or you, right?

Based on this list, it seems you and I have a lot in common with Jesus.

Big deal? I think so.

Jesus understands you. He understands small-town anonymity and big-city pressure. He's walked through pastures of sheep and palaces of kings. He's faced hunger, sorrow, and death and wants to face them with you. Jesus "understands our weaknesses, for he faced all of the same testings we do, yet he did not sin" (Hebrews 4:15 NLT).

If Jesus understands our weaknesses, then so does God. Jesus was God in human form. He was God with us. That is why Jesus is called Immanuel.

> If Jesus understands our weaknesses, then so does God.

Immanuel appears in the same Hebrew form as it did two thousand years ago. *Immanu* means "with us." *El* refers to

Elohim, or God. So Immanuel is not an "above-us God" or a "somewhere-in-the-neighborhood God." He came as the "with-us God." God with us. Not "God with the rich" or "God with the religious." But God with *us*. All of us. Russians, Germans, Buddhists, Mormons, truck drivers and taxi drivers, librarians. God with *us*.

Don't we love the word *with*? Especially when we feel lonely. "Will you go *with* me?" we ask. "To the store, to the hospital, through my life?" God says he will. "I am *with* you always," Jesus said before he ascended to heaven, "to the very end of the age" (Matthew 28:20 NIV). Search for restrictions on the promise; you'll find none. You won't find "I'll be with you if you behave . . . when you believe. I'll be with you on Sundays in worship . . . at Mass." No, none of that. There's no withholding tax on God's "with" promise. He is *with* us.

God is with us.

Prophets weren't enough. Apostles wouldn't do. Angels won't suffice. God sent more than miracles and messages. He sent himself; he sent his Son. "The Word became flesh and dwelt among us" (John 1:14).

> God sent more than
> miracles and messages.
> He sent himself; he
> sent his Son.

And because Jesus understands, we can go to him.

Wouldn't his lack of understanding keep us from him? Doesn't the lack of understanding keep us from others? Suppose you were discouraged because of your financial state and needed some guidance from a sympathetic friend. Would you go to the son of a zillionaire? (Remember, you're asking for guidance, not a handout.) Would you approach someone who inherited a fortune? Probably not. Why? He would not understand. He's likely never been where you are, so he can't relate to how you feel.

Jesus, however, has and can. He has been where you are and can relate to how you feel. And if his life on earth doesn't convince you, his death on the cross should. He understands what you are going through. Our Lord does not patronize us or scoff at our needs. He responds "generously to all without finding fault" (James 1:5 NIV). How can he do this? No one penned it more clearly than the author of Hebrews.

Jesus understands every weakness of ours, because he was tempted in every way that we are. But he did not sin! So whenever we are in need, we should come bravely before the throne of our merciful God. There we will be treated with undeserved kindness, and we will find help. (Hebrews 4:15–16 CEV)

For thirty-three years he felt everything you and I have felt. He felt weak. He grew weary. He was afraid of failure. He was susceptible to wooing women. He got colds, burped, and had body odor. His feelings got hurt. His feet got tired. And his head ached.

To think of Jesus in such a light is . . . well, it seems almost irreverent, doesn't it? It's not something we like to do; it's uncomfortable. It is much easier to keep the humanity out of the incarnation. Clean the manure from around the manger. Wipe the sweat out of his eyes. Pretend he never snored or blew his nose or hit his thumb with a hammer.

He's easier to handle that way. Something about keeping him divine also keeps him distant, packaged, predictable.

But don't do it. For heaven's sake don't. Let him be as human as he intended to be. Let him into the mire and muck of our world, for only if we let him in can he pull us out.

Reflection

Spend some time reflecting on what you have read by journaling your thoughts and answers to the following prompts and questions.

1. Describe a time when you felt lonely. That time could be now or sometime in the past. What made you feel lonely? What was the hardest part of feeling lonely?

_____

_____

_____

_____

2. What does the word *Immanuel* mean, and why is this
   word important for us to understand?

   _____

   _____

   _____

   _____

   _____

3. Have you ever thought about turning to Jesus during
   your loneliness? Why or why not?

   _____

   _____

   _____

   _____

   _____

4. How could the promise of Immanuel help you feel less alone right now?

_____

_____

_____

God's Word for You

Allow these passages from God's Word to remind you that God will help you when you feel lonely.

"And surely I am with you always, to the very end of the age."

MATTHEW 28:20 NIV

Note how Jesus emphasizes this promise using the word surely.

Even though I walk through the darkest valley,
    I fear no evil;
for you are with me;
      your rod and your staff—
      they comfort me.

PSALM 23:4 NRSV

God's presence rids us of fear and comforts our souls.

"And I will ask the Father, and he will give you another advocate to help you and be with you forever—the Spirit of truth."

JOHN 14:16–17 NIV

Our advocate is the Holy Spirit—our helper who is always with us so that we are never alone.

Read the following prayer, silently or aloud. When you have finished praying, spend a moment in silence, listening for the voice of God.

Heavenly Father, I need the promise of Immanuel today. I need to know you are with me. Sometimes I feel so alone. I feel like I don't have any friends. I feel like my family doesn't understand me. I feel like I have no one to turn to. In those moments, remind me to turn to you and to your son, Jesus, who came to earth because you wanted to be close to us. In Christ, I know you are always near. You don't go anywhere. When I am all alone, I can cry out to you, and you will hear me because you are always close by. And because of Jesus you understand me. Thank you for the comfort I have in that promise. In Jesus' name, amen.

CHAPTER 6

God Will Help You in Your Everyday Life

*J*esus was attending a wedding with the disciples and his mother, Mary, when she approached him with a strange and seemingly irrelevant problem. "They have no more wine," she told him (John 2:3 NIV).

Had I been the angel on call that day, I would have intervened. I would have placed a wing between Mary and Jesus and reminded her about the mission of her Son. "He was not sent to the earth to handle such mundane, day-to-day tasks. We are saving his miraculous powers for cadaver calling, leper touching, and demon casting. No wine? Don't whine to Jesus."

But I was not the angel on call. And Mary enlisted the help of her Son to deal with the problem: empty wine ladles. Folks in first-century Palestine knew how to throw a party. None of this wedding and reception in one evening, no sir.

Weddings lasted as long as seven days. Food and wine were expected to last just as long. So Mary was concerned when she saw the servants scraping the bottom of the wine barrel.

Fault poor planning by the wedding planner. Fault guests for guzzling more than their share. Fault Jesus for showing up with a troop of thirsty disciples. We are not told the reason for the shortage. But we are told how it was replenished. Mary presented the problem. Christ was reluctant. Mary deferred. Jesus reconsidered. He commanded. The servants obeyed and offered the sommelier what they could have sworn was water. He sipped, licked his lips, held the glass up to the light, and said something about their squirreling away the best wine for the farewell toasts. The servants escorted him across the room to see the six vats filled to the brim with fruit of the vine. The wineless wedding was suddenly wine flush. Mary smiled at her Son. Jesus raised a glass to his mother, and we are left with this message: our diminishing supplies, no matter how insignificant, matter to heaven.

I have a curious testimony to this truth. During one of my many less-than-sane seasons of life, I competed in Half

Ironman Triathlons. The event consists of a 1.2-mile swim, a 56-mile bike ride, and a 13.1-mile run. Why was a fifty-year-old preacher participating in such endeavors? That's what my wife kept asking me. (Don't worry. I didn't wear a Speedo.)

During one of these races, I prayed the oddest prayer of my life. Four of us traveled to Florida for the race. One of my friends had invited a competitor from Indiana to join us. All told, I knew these three participants. There were at least two hundred people whom I did not know, a fact that proved crucial to my story.

I finished the swim, if not dead last, at least nearly dead and almost last. I mounted my bike and began the three-hour trek. About a third of the way into the cycling portion, I reached into the pocket of my shirt to grab some GU. GU is a packet of easily eaten essential nutrients. Well, guess who forgot his GU? I was GU-less with a good thirty miles to go. One doesn't find any GU-selling convenience stores on the triathlon road.

So I prayed. Between puffs and pedal strokes, I said,

"Lord, this very well might be the only time in eternity you've heard this request. But here is my situation . . ."

Did GU fall from heaven? Well, sort of. The fellow from Indiana, the friend of my friend, one of the three people I knew out of the entire field, just "happened" to pedal up from behind me.

"Hey, Max, how's it going?" he asked.

"Well, I have a problem."

When he heard of my GU-lessness, he reached into the pocket of his biking shirt, pulled out three packs, and said, "I've got plenty!" He handed them to me, and off he went.

You may very well be thinking, *Lucado, that is a lame example of answered prayer. I'm dealing with disease, debt, the threat of layoffs and letdowns, and you're talking about something as lightweight as GU in a race?*

That's precisely my point.

Indeed, I think that is Jesus' point. Of what import is a wineless wedding? Of all the needs of people on the planet, why would bone-dry wine vats matter? Simple. It mattered to Jesus because it mattered to Mary. If Jesus was willing to use divine clout to solve a social faux pas, how much more willing would he be to intervene on the weightier matters of life?

He wants you to know that you can take your needs—all your needs—to him. "Be anxious for nothing, but *in everything* by prayer and supplication, with thanksgiving, let your requests be made known to God" (Philippians 4:6, emphasis mine).

In everything—not just the big things—let your requests be made known.

Mary modeled this. She presented the need to Christ. "They have no more wine." No fanfare. No drama. She knew the problem. She knew the provider. She connected the first with the second.

So I ask, Have you asked? Have you turned your deficit into a prayer? Jesus will tailor a response to your precise need. He is not a fast-food cook. He is an accomplished chef who prepares unique blessings for unique situations. When crowds of people came to Christ for healing, "*One by one he placed his hands on them and healed them*" (Luke 4:40 MSG, emphasis mine).

Had Jesus chosen to do so, he could have proclaimed a cloud of healing blessings to fall on the crowd. But he is not a one-size-fits-all Savior. He placed his hands on each one, individually, personally. Perceiving unique needs, he issued unique blessings.

A precise prayer gives Christ the opportunity to remove all doubt about his love and interest. Your problem becomes his pathway. The challenge you face becomes a canvas on which Christ can demonstrate his finest work. So offer a simple prayer and entrust the problem to Christ.

We all know what it's like to offer that prayer only to receive silence in return. It's important to note in this miracle, Jesus hesitated at first: "Dear woman, that's not our problem . . . My time has not yet come" (John 2:4 NLT).

You've heard the same. In your personal version of verse three, you explained your shortage: no more wine, time, vigor, or vision. Your needle was on empty; the tank had run dry; the bank account was showing a negative balance. You pleaded your case in verse three. And then came verse four. Silence. Quiet as a library at midnight. The reply did not come. No deficit-erasing deposit was made. When no answer comes, how does your verse five read? "His mother told the servants, 'Do whatever he tells you'" (John 2:5 NLT). Translation? "Jesus is in charge. I'm not." "He runs the world. I don't." "He sees the future. I can't." "I trust Jesus. Whatever he tells you to do, do it."

Something in the explicit faith of Mary caused Jesus to change his agenda.

> Standing nearby were six stone water jars, used for Jewish ceremonial washing. Each could hold twenty to thirty gallons. Jesus told the servants, "Fill the jars with water." When the jars had been filled, he said, "Now dip some out, and take it to the master of ceremonies." So the servants followed his instructions. (vv. 6–8 NLT)

Six water jars would create enough wine for—hang on to your hat—756 bottles of wine![1] Napa never knew such a harvest.

When the master of ceremonies tasted the water that was now wine, not knowing where it had come from (though, of course, the servants knew), he called the bridegroom over. "A host always serves the best wine first," he said. "Then, when everyone has had a lot to drink, he brings out the less expensive wine. But you have kept the best until now!" (vv. 9–10 NLT)

The miracle of Christ resulted in not just an abundance of wine but the abundance of good wine. Cooking wine would have sufficed. Convenience-store vintage would have met the expectations of the guests. A modest sip-with-pizza-on-a-Tuesday-night quaff would have been enough for Mary. But it was not enough for Jesus. Something powerful happens when we present our needs to him and trust him to do what is right: he is "able to do exceedingly abundantly above all that we ask or think" (Ephesians 3:20).

It simply falls to us to believe—to believe that Jesus is King of each and every situation. So make your specific request, and trust him to do not what you want but what is best. Before you know it, you'll be raising a toast in honor of the One who hears your requests.

Reflection

Spend some time reflecting on what you have read by journaling your thoughts and answers to the following prompts and questions.

1. If you had been a bystander at the wedding in Cana, what would you have thought of Mary's request of Jesus and why?

_____

_____

_____

_____

_____

Compared to the other miracles Jesus performed during his ministry, such as restoring sight to a blind man and raising a girl from the dead, how do you think this miracle compares? Why do you think it's recorded in the gospels?

_____

_____

_____

2. What is the "smallest" prayer you've ever prayed, a prayer for something seemingly insignificant? Was the prayer answered? If so, how? If not, how did you respond to God's silence?

_____

_____

_____

_____

Do you believe that "our diminishing supplies, no matter how insignificant, matter to heaven"? Why or why not?

_____

_____

_____

_____

3. Use the space below to list some ordinary, everyday things you feel anxious about or need prayer for.

_____

_____

_____

_____

_____

_____

How do you feel about offering this list to God in prayer?

_____

_____

God's Word for You

Allow these passages from God's Word to remind you that God will help you in your everyday life.

"Therefore do not worry, saying, 'What shall we eat?' or 'What shall we drink?' or 'What shall we wear?' For after all these things the Gentiles seek. For your heavenly Father knows that you need all these things. But seek first the kingdom of God and His righteousness, and all these things shall be added to you. Therefore do not worry about tomorrow, for tomorrow will worry about its own things. Sufficient for the day is its own trouble."

MATTHEW 6:31–34

God knows what you need for each day, and he will provide it.

> Trust in the LORD with all your heart
>> and lean not on your own understanding;
> in all your ways submit to him,
>> and he will make your paths straight.

PROVERBS 3:5–6 NIV

In how many ways are we to submit to God? All. The small, the big, and everything in between.

For we do not have a high priest who is unable to empathize with our weaknesses, but we have one who has been tempted in every way, just as we are—yet he did not sin. Let us then approach God's throne of grace with confidence, so that we may receive mercy and find grace to help us in our time of need.

HEBREWS 4:15–16 NIV

Because of Jesus, we can approach God's throne with any request and know we will receive mercy and understanding.

Pray through the list you made in question three, and then read the following prayer, silently or aloud. When you have finished praying, spend a moment in silence, listening for the voice of God.

God, I offer this list of worries and concerns to you. I don't always believe that you care about the ordinary parts of my life, but I know that in any relationship, communicating about the small things is important. So, Lord, I lay these small things down at your feet. I entrust them to you. May this offering deepen our relationship. May it teach me to trust you with the big and small parts of my life. Even if I don't get the answers that I want, thank you for listening and caring about my needs, even the ordinary ones. In Jesus' name I pray, amen.

CHAPTER 7

God Will Help You When You Are Sick

We don't know her name, but we know her situation. Her world was midnight black. Grope-in-the-dark-and-hope-for-help black. Read these three verses and see what I mean:

> A large crowd followed Jesus and pushed very close around him. Among them was a woman who had been bleeding for twelve years. She had suffered very much from many doctors and had spent all the money she had, but instead of improving, she was getting worse. (Mark 5:24–26 NCV)

She was a bruised reed: "bleeding for twelve years," "suffered very much," "spent all the money she had," and "getting worse." She was physically exhausted and socially ostracized. She awoke daily in a body that no one wanted. She was down to her last prayer. And on the day we encounter her, she's about to pray it.

Perhaps you have felt this way. You've been sick for days, weeks, years. Doctors, specialists, tests—no one seems to know the cure, and you are tired. You are tired of being sick, but most of all you are tired of hoping. Each day you hope and pray today will be better than the last, and each day you are disappointed. How do you continue to believe you will be healed? How do you continue to believe that God cares?

By the time the woman in our story gets to Jesus, he is surrounded by people. He's on his way to help the daughter of Jairus, one of the most important men in the community. What are the odds that he will interrupt an urgent mission with a high official to help the likes of her? Still, she takes a chance.

"If I can just touch his clothes," she thinks, "I will be healed" (v. 28 NCV). It was her last hope, her last resort. Her last-ditch effort in a long series of efforts to be made well, and it all depended on this man they were calling a prophet. It all depended on Jesus.

Risky decision. To touch him she will have to touch the people. If one of them recognizes her, hello rebuke, goodbye cure. But what choice does she have? She has no money, no clout, no friends, no solutions. All she has is a crazy hunch that Jesus can help and a final hope that he will.

> It all depended on Jesus.

Maybe that's all you have: a crazy hunch and a little bit of hope. You have nothing to give. But you are hurting. And all you have to offer him is your hurt.

Maybe that has kept you from coming to God. Oh, you've taken a step or two in his direction. But then you saw the other people around him. They seemed so clean, so neat, so trim and fit in their faith. And when you saw them, they blocked your view of him. So you stepped back.

If that describes you, note carefully that only one person was commended that day for having faith. It wasn't a wealthy giver. It wasn't a loyal follower. It was a shame-struck, penniless outcast who clutched on to her hunch that he could help and her hope that he would.

Which, by the way, isn't a bad definition of faith: *a conviction that he can and a hope that he will.* Sounds similar to the definition of faith given in the Bible: "Without faith no one can please God. Anyone who comes to God must believe that he is real and that he rewards those who truly want to find him" (Hebrews 11:6 NCV).

A healthy woman never would have appreciated the power of a touch of the hem of his robe. But this woman was sick, and when her dilemma met his dedication, a miracle occurred. Her part in the healing was very small. All she did was extend her arm through the crowd.

> When her dilemma met his dedication, a miracle occurred.

"If only I can touch him."

What's important is not the form of the effort but the fact of the effort. The fact is, she did something. She refused to settle for sickness another day and resolved to make a move.

Healing begins when we do something. Healing begins when we reach out. Healing starts when we take a step of faith.

God's help is near and always available, but it is given only to those who seek it. The great work in this story is the mighty healing that occurred. But the great truth is that the healing began with her touch. And with that small, courageous gesture, she experienced Jesus' tender power. "Jesus turned around, and when He saw her He said, 'Be of good cheer, daughter; your faith has made you well.' And the woman was made well from that hour" (Matthew 9:22).

If you are low on faith but need the healing power of Christ, perhaps you could rely on the faith of a friend. This is the type of faith Jesus witnessed when he saw a man being lowered through a hole in the roof where Jesus was teaching one day (Mark 2:1–12).

Whether he was born paralyzed or became paralyzed, we don't know, but the end result was the same: total dependence on others. Perhaps someone had to wash his face and bathe his body. He couldn't go on a walk or run an errand on his own.

When people looked at him, they didn't see the man; they saw a body in need of a miracle. That's not what Jesus saw, but that's what the people saw. And that's certainly what his friends saw. So they did what any of us would do for a friend. They tried to get him some help.

Word was out that a carpenter-turned-teacher-turned-wonder-worker was in town. By the time his friends arrived at the place, the house was full. People jammed the doorways. Kids sat in the windows. Others peeked over shoulders. How would this small band of friends ever attract Jesus' attention?

> Word was out that a carpenter-turned-teacher-turned-wonder-worker was in town.

They had to make a choice: do we go in or give up?

What would have happened had the friends given up faith? What if they had shrugged their shoulders and mumbled something about the crowd being big and dinner getting cold and had turned and left? After all, they had done a good deed in coming this far. Who could fault them for turning back? You can do only so much for somebody. But these friends hadn't done enough.

One said he had an idea. The four huddled over the paralytic and discussed the plan to climb to the top of the house, cut through the roof, and lower their friend down with their sashes.

It was risky—they could fall. It was dangerous—he could fall. It was unorthodox—de-roofing is antisocial. It was intrusive—Jesus was busy. But it was their only chance to see Jesus. So they climbed to the roof.

Faith does those things. Faith does the unexpected. And faith gets God's attention. Look what Mark says: "When Jesus saw the faith of these people, he said to the paralyzed man, 'Young man, your sins are forgiven'" (Mark 2:5 NCV).

Finally, someone took Jesus at his word! Four men had enough hope in him and love for their friend that they took a chance. The stretcher above was a sign from above—somebody believed! Someone was willing to risk embarrassment and injury for just a few moments with the Galilean.

Jesus was moved by the scene of faith.

The request of the friends was valid—but timid. The expectations of the crowd were high—but not high enough. They expected Jesus to say, "I heal you." Instead he said, "I forgive you."

They expected him to treat the body, for that is what they saw.

He chose to treat not only the body but also the spirit, for that is what he saw.

They wanted Jesus to give the man a new body so he could walk. Jesus gave grace so the man could live. "And they were all amazed, and they glorified God" (Luke 5:26).

> He chose to treat not only the body but also the spirit, for that is what he saw.

Two pictures of miracle-prompting faith: A woman who reached out. Friends who drew near. Jesus responded both times. He did the impossible for them. He will do the same for you. And you know what the best news is? Jesus heals the body, but he also heals the soul. He sees you as more than just an ailing body. He sees that your heart, mind, and soul need healing too. He offers more than you ask because he knows exactly what you need. Come to him, have faith, and he will make you well.

Reflection

Spend some time reflecting on what you have read by journaling your thoughts and answers to the following prompts and questions.

1. What needs healing in your life right now? Your health, your heart, a relationship? Describe it below.

_____

_____

_____

What has been the most difficult part of this sickness or brokenness?

_____

_____

_____

_____

2. How can you relate to the woman in Mark 5 who touched Jesus' garment in an attempt to be made well? Have you ever felt desperate for healing the way she did? If so, where have you gone to seek it?

_____

_____

_____

_____

_____

3. The Gospel of Mark also tells the story of a group of men who helped their friend who was a paralytic. Has your community ever helped you during a time of need? If so, what was that experience like?

_____

_____

_____

_____

_____

_____

_____

_____

_____

_____

Thinking back to your answer for question one, what would it look like for you to reach out to your community for help and support in the midst of this sickness or brokenness?

_____

_____

_____

_____

What would it look like for you to reach out to Jesus?

_____

_____

_____

_____

_____

God's Word for You

Allow these passages from God's Word to remind you that God will help you if you are sick.

"Jesus turned around, and when He saw her He said, 'Be of good cheer, daughter; your faith has made you well.' And the woman was made well from that hour."

MATTHEW 9:22

Our faith makes us well, whether that is in our bodies or our spirits. Faith is hope.

"Come to Me, all you who labor and are heavy laden, and I will give you rest. Take My yoke upon you and learn from Me, for I am gentle and lowly in heart, and you will find rest for your souls. For My yoke is easy and My burden is light."

MATTHEW 11:28–30

No matter your ailment, Jesus offers you rest. Let him carry whatever is weighing you down.

"They will be his people, and God himself will be with them and be their God. 'He will wipe every tear from their eyes. There will be no more death' or mourning or crying or pain, for the old order of things has passed away."

REVELATION 21:3–4 NIV

Ultimately, God's plan is for everyone to be healed. His promise for eternity is no more death, crying, or pain.

Read the following prayer, silently or aloud. When you have finished praying, spend a moment in silence, listening for the voice of God.

God, I know that you are my healer. You are the miracle worker. You can heal every sickness and disease. You can raise the dead to life. I confess it is easier for me to believe you can heal others than it is to believe you will heal me. It makes me feel vulnerable to trust you with my sickness and brokenness. I don't want to get my hopes up and then be disappointed. At the same time, I don't want to lose hope. Help me believe in your healing powers. Strengthen my faith in you, your power to heal me, and your love for me. Give me the courage to reach out to friends and family for help. May I encounter the healing powers of my Lord Jesus. May I believe again. Lord, make me well. In Christ I pray, amen.

CHAPTER 8

God Will Help You Get Through Grief

*W*e don't discuss graveyards to brighten our day. Cemeteries aren't typically known for their inspiration. But an exception was found in a graveyard near Bethany. And that one exception is exceptional.

A man named Lazarus was sick. He lived in Bethany with his sisters, Mary and Martha. This is the Mary who later poured the expensive perfume on the Lord's feet and wiped them with her hair. Her brother, Lazarus, was sick. So the two sisters sent a message to Jesus telling him, "Lord, your dear friend is very sick." (John 11:1–3 NLT)

John weighted the opening words of the chapter with reality: "A man named Lazarus was sick." Your journal might reveal a comparable statement. "A woman named

Judy was tired." "A father named Tom was confused." "A youngster named Sophia was sad."

Lazarus was a real person with a real problem. He was sick; his body ached; his fever raged; his stomach churned. But he had something going for him. Or, better stated, he had Someone going for him. He had a friend named Jesus, the water-to-wine, stormy-sea-to-calm-waters, picnic-basket-to-buffet Jesus. Others were fans of Christ. Lazarus was friends with him.

So the sisters of Lazarus sent Jesus a not-too-subtle message: "Lord, your dear friend is very sick."

They appealed to the love of Jesus and stated their problem. They did not tell him how to respond. No presumption. No overreaching or underreacting. They simply wrapped their concern in a sentence and left it with Jesus. A lesson for us perhaps?

> Others were fans of Christ. Lazarus was friends with him.

Christ responded to the crisis of health with a promise of help. "But when Jesus heard about it he said, 'Lazarus's sickness will not end in death. No, it happened for the glory of God so that the Son of God will receive glory from this'" (John 11:4 NLT).

It would have been easy to misunderstand this promise. The listener could be forgiven for hearing "Lazarus will not face death or endure death." But Jesus made a different promise: "This sickness will not end in death." Lazarus, we learn, would find himself in the valley of death, but he would not stay there.

The messenger surely hurried back to Bethany and told the family to take heart and have hope.

Yet "he [Jesus] stayed where he was for the next two days" (v. 6 NLT).

The crisis of health was exacerbated by the crisis of delay. How many times did Lazarus ask his sisters, "Is Jesus here yet?" How many times did they mop his fevered brow and then look for Jesus' coming? Did they not assure one another, "Any minute now Jesus will arrive"? But days came and went. No Jesus. Lazarus began to fade. No Jesus. Lazarus died. No Jesus.

"When Jesus arrived at Bethany, he was told that Lazarus had already been in his grave for four days" (John 11:17 NLT). "Israel's rabbinic faith taught that for three days a soul lingered about a body, but on the fourth day it left permanently."[1] Jesus was a day late, or so it seemed.

The sisters thought he was. "When Martha got word that Jesus was coming, she went to meet him. But Mary stayed in the house. Martha said to Jesus, 'Lord, if only you had been here, my brother would not have died'" (vv. 20–21 NLT).

She was disappointed in Jesus. "If only you had been here." Christ did not meet her expectations. By the time Jesus arrived, Lazarus had been dead for the better part of a week. In our day his body would have been embalmed or cremated, the obituary would have been printed, the burial plot purchased, and the funeral at least planned, if not completed.

I know this to be true because I've planned many funerals. And in more memorials than I can count, I've told the Lazarus story. I've even dared to stand near the casket, look into the faces of modern-day Marthas, Marys, Matthews, and Michaels and say, "Maybe you, like Martha, are disappointed. You told Jesus about the sickness. You waited at the hospital bed. You kept vigil in the convalescent room. You told him that the one he loved was sick, sicker, dying. And now death has come. And some of you find yourselves, like Mary, too bereaved to speak. Others, like Martha, too bewildered to be silent. Would you be willing to imitate the faith of Martha?"

Look again at her words: "Lord, *if only* you had been here, my brother would not have died. But *even now I know* that God will give you whatever you ask" (vv. 21–22 NLT, emphasis mine). How much time do you suppose passed between the "if only" of verse 21 and the "even now I know" of verse 22? What caused the change in her tone? Did she see something in the expression of Christ? Did she remember a promise from the past? Did his hand brush

> Would you be willing to imitate the faith of Martha?

away her tear? Did his confidence calm her fear? Something moved Martha from complaint to confession.

Jesus responded with a death-defying promise: "Jesus told her, 'Your brother will rise again.' 'Yes,' Martha said, 'he will rise when everyone else rises, at the last day.' Jesus told her, 'I am the resurrection and the life. Anyone who believes in me will live, even after dying. . . . Do you believe this?'" (vv. 23–26 NLT).

The moment drips with drama.

Look to whom Jesus asked this question: a bereaved, heartbroken sister.

Look at where Jesus stood as he asked this question: within the vicinity, perhaps in the center, of a cemetery.

Look at when Jesus asked this question: four days too late. Lazarus, his friend, was four days dead, four days gone, four days buried.

Martha has had plenty of time to give up on Jesus. Yet now this Jesus has the audacity to pull rank over death and ask, "Do you believe this, Martha? Do you believe that I am Lord of all, even of the cemetery?" Maybe she answered with a lilt in her voice, with the conviction of a triumphant angel, fists pumping the air and face radiant with hope. Give her reply a dozen exclamation marks if you want, but I don't. I hear a pause, a swallow. I hear a meek "Yes, Lord, . . . I have always believed you are the Messiah, the Son of God, the one who has come into the world from God" (v. 27 NLT).

Martha wasn't ready to say Jesus could raise the dead. Even so, she gave him a triple tribute: "the Messiah," "the Son of God," and "the one who has come into the world." She mustered a mustard-seed confession. That was enough for Jesus.

Martha fetched her sister. Mary saw Christ and wept. And "when Jesus saw her weeping and saw the other people wailing with her, a deep anger welled up within him, and he was deeply troubled. 'Where have you put him?' he asked them. They told him, 'Lord, come and see.' Then Jesus wept" (vv. 33–35 NLT).

What caused Jesus to weep? Did he cry at the death of his friend? Or the impact death had on his friends? Did he weep out of sorrow? Or anger? Was it the fact of the grave or its control over people that broke his heart?

It must have been the latter because a determined, not despondent, Jesus took charge. Jesus told them to roll the stone away. Martha hesitated. Who wouldn't? He insisted. She complied. Then came the command, no doubt the only command ever made to a cadaver. Jesus, prone as he was to thank God for impossible situations, offered a prayer of gratitude, and "then Jesus shouted, 'Lazarus, come out!' And the dead man came out, his hands and feet bound in graveclothes, his face wrapped in a headcloth. Jesus told them, 'Unwrap him and let him go!'" (vv. 43–44 NLT).

"Don't miss the message of this miracle," I love to say at funerals, although careful not to get too animated, because, after all, it is a memorial service. Still, I indulge in some excitement. "You are never alone. Jesus meets us in the cemeteries of life. Whether we are there to say goodbye or there to be buried, we can count on the presence of God."

He is "Lord both of the dead and of the living" (Romans 14:9 ESV). An encore is scheduled. Lazarus was but a warm-up. Jesus will someday shout, and the ingathering of saints will begin. Graveyards, ocean depths, battlefields, burned buildings, and every other resting place of the

> You are never alone. Jesus meets us in the cemeteries of life.

deceased will give up the dead in whatever condition they might be found. They will be recomposed, resurrected, and re-presented in the presence of Christ. Salvation of the saints is not merely the redemption of souls but also the recollection of souls and bodies.

When we are in Christ, we grieve, but we grieve with hope. Lazarus is proof of this. His death proved that our Savior grieves death with us. Jesus cares and understands and feels the weight of death just like we do. But as the conqueror of death, Jesus knows death is not the end. It is simply the beginning of a life we cannot imagine during our lives on earth. So grieve here, today. Receive the comfort of Christ in your sorrow, but hold fast to the promise that the sorrow you feel in the night makes way for joy in the morning.

Reflection

Spend some time reflecting on what you have read by journaling your thoughts and answers to the following prompts and questions.

1. When we think of grieving, we often think of the grief that follows death. But you can grieve many things: a dream, a relationship that has ended, an old home or city you moved away from. What are you grieving today, or what have you grieved most recently? What has your grieving process looked like?

   _____

   _____

   _____

   _____

   _____

2. In the story of Lazarus's resurrection, Jesus was sad that his friend had died. How does it feel to know Jesus also experienced grief?

_____

_____

_____

_____

Write down the thoughts or questions you have for Jesus about what you are grieving right now. Be honest with him. Remember, he has felt what you feel.

_____

_____

_____

_____

_____

3. How have you experienced hope in the midst of grief, either in the season of grief you are in now or grief you've experienced in the past?

_____

_____

_____

_____

God's Word for You

Allow these passages from God's Word to remind you that God will help you when you are grieving.

> Weeping may endure for a night,
> But joy comes in the morning.
>
> PSALM 30:5

Grief is not forever; it is a season.

> He heals the brokenhearted
> And binds up their wounds.
> He counts the number of the stars;
> He calls them all by name.
> Great is our Lord, and mighty in power;
> His understanding is infinite.
>
> PSALM 147:3–5

There is no pain God does not understand.

> "Blessed are the poor in spirit,
> For theirs is the kingdom of heaven.
> Blessed are those who mourn,
> For they shall be comforted."
>
> MATTHEW 5:3–4

Those who mourn are blessed by the comfort of Jesus.

Read the following prayer, silently or aloud. When you have finished praying, spend a moment in silence, listening for the voice of God.

Father, I know you are my comforter. I know you are strong when I am weak. I know you are hope when I am hopeless. I need all these from you today—comfort, strength, and hope—because I cannot muster them on my own. When I am deep in grief, all I see is darkness, and all I feel is hopeless. But you empathize with this pain. You know it well. Remind me of your love during this time. Remind me that I can share my thoughts and struggles with you. You are not afraid of negative feelings. Hold me as I walk through this season of grief. Don't let me run away from it, but also don't let me fall into despair. Guide me toward the hope and light I have in Christ. In his name, amen.

CHAPTER 9

God Will Help
You with Guidance

If only we could order life the way we order gourmet coffee. Wouldn't you love to mix and match the ingredients of your future?

"Give me a tall, extra-hot cup of adventure, cut the dangers, with two shots of good health."

"A decaf brew of longevity, please, with a sprinkle of fertility. Go heavy on the agility and cut the disability."

"I'll have a pleasure mocha with extra stirrings of indulgence. Make sure it's consequence free."

"I'll go with a grande happy-latte, with a dollop of love, sprinkled with Caribbean retirement."

Take me to that coffee shop. Too bad it doesn't exist. Truth is, life often hands us a concoction entirely different from the one we requested. Ever feel as though the barista-from-above called your name and handed you a cup of unwanted stress?

"Joe Jones, enjoy your early retirement. Looks as if it comes with marital problems and inflation."

"Mary Adams, you wanted four years of university education, then kids. You'll be having kids first. Congratulations on your pregnancy."

"A hot cup of job transfer six months before your daughter's graduation, Susie. Would you like some patience with that?"

Life comes caffeinated with surprises. Modifications. Transitions. Alterations. You move down the ladder, out of the house, over for the new guy, up through the system. All this moving. Some changes welcome, others not. And in those rare seasons when you think the world has settled down, watch out. One seventy-seven-year-old recently told a friend of mine, "I've had a good life. I am enjoying my life now, and I am looking forward to the future." Two weeks later

> "I'll go with a grande happy-latte, with a dollop of love, sprinkled with Caribbean retirement."

a tornado ripped through the region, taking the lives of his son, daughter-in-law, grandson, and daughter-in-law's mother. We just don't know, do we? On our list of fears, the fear of what's next demands a prominent position. We might request a decaffeinated life, but we don't get it. The disciples didn't.

"I am going away" (John 14:28).

Imagine their shock when they heard Jesus say those words. He spoke them on the night of the Passover celebration, Thursday evening, in the upper room. Christ and his friends had just enjoyed a calm dinner in the midst of a chaotic week. They had reason for optimism: Jesus' popularity was soaring. Opportunities were increasing. In three short years the crowds had lifted Christ to their shoulders . . . he was the hope of the common man.

The disciples were talking kingdom rhetoric, ready to rain down fire on their enemies, jockeying for positions in the cabinet of Christ. They envisioned a restoration of Israel to her days of glory. No more Roman occupation or foreign oppression. This was the parade to freedom, and Jesus was leading it.

And now this? Jesus said, "I am going away." The announcement stunned them. When Jesus explained, "You know the way to where I am going," Thomas, with no small dose of exasperation, replied, "No, we don't know, Lord. . . . We have no idea where you are going, so how can we know the way?" (John 14:4–5 NLT). Christ handed the disciples a cup of major transition, and they tried to hand it back. Wouldn't we do the same? Yet who succeeds? What person passes through life surprise free? If you don't want change, go to a soda machine; that's the only place you won't find any. Remember the summary of Solomon?

> This was the parade to freedom, and Jesus was leading it.

> For everything there is a season,
> a time for every activity under heaven. (Ecclesiastes 3:1 NLT)

If you continue to read the next seven verses, you would count twenty-eight different seasons. Birth, death, lamenting, cheering, loving, hating, embracing, separating. God dispenses life the way he manages his cosmos: through seasons. When it comes to the earth, we understand God's management strategy. Nature needs winter to rest and spring to awaken. We don't dash into underground shelters at the sight of spring's tree buds. Autumn colors don't prompt warning sirens. Earthly seasons don't upset us. But unexpected personal ones certainly do. The way we panic at the sight of change, you'd think bombs were falling on Iowa.

"Run for your lives! Graduation is coming!"

"The board of directors just hired a new CEO. Take cover!"

"Load the women and children into the bus, and head north. The department store is going out of business!"

Change trampolines our lives, and when it does, God sends someone special to stabilize us.

On the eve of his death, Jesus gave his followers this promise: "When the Father sends the Advocate as my representative—that is, the Holy Spirit—he will teach you everything and will remind you of everything I have told you. I am leaving you with a gift—peace of mind and heart. And the peace I give is a gift the world cannot give. So don't be troubled or afraid" (John 14:26–27 NLT).

> Change trampolines our lives, and when it does, God sends someone special to stabilize us.

As a departing teacher might introduce the classroom to her replacement, so Jesus introduces us to the Holy Spirit. And what a ringing endorsement he gives. Jesus calls the Holy Spirit his "representative." The Spirit comes in the name of Christ, with equal authority and identical power. Earlier in the evening Jesus had said, "I will ask the Father, and he will give you another Counselor to be with you forever" (John 14:16 CSB).

"Another Counselor." Both words shimmer. The Greek

language enjoys two distinct words for *another*. One means "totally different," and the second translates "another just like the first one." When Jesus promises "another Counselor," he uses word number two, promising "another just like the first one."

The distinction is instructive. Let's say you are reading a book as you ride on a bus. Someone takes the seat next to yours, interrupts your reading, and inquires about the book. You tell him, "Max Lucado wrote it. Here, take it. I can get another."

When you say, "I can get another," do you mean "another" in the sense of "any other" book? A crime novel, cookbook, or a romance paperback? Of course not. Being a person of exquisite taste, you mean a book that is identical to the one you so kindly gave away. If you had been speaking Greek, you would have used the term John used in recording Jesus' promise: *allos*—"Another one just like the first one."

And who was the first one? Jesus himself. Hence, the assurance Jesus gave to the disciples was this: "I am going away. You are entering a new season, a different chapter. Much will be different, but one thing remains constant: my presence. You will enjoy the presence of 'another Counselor.'"

Counselor means "friend" (MSG), "helper" (NKJV), "intercessor, advocate, strengthener, and standby" (AMPC). All descriptors attempt to portray the beautiful meaning of *parakletos*, a compound of two Greek words. *Para* means "alongside of" (think of "parallel" or "paradox"). *Kletos* means "to be called out, designated, assigned, or appointed."

> The Holy Spirit is designated to come alongside you.

The Holy Spirit is designated to come alongside you. He is the presence of Jesus with and in the followers of Jesus.

Can you see how the disciples needed this encouragement? It's Thursday night before the crucifixion. By Friday's sunrise they will abandon Jesus. The breakfast hour will find them hiding in corners and crevices. At 9 a.m., Roman soldiers will nail Christ to a cross. By this time tomorrow he will be dead and buried. Their world is about to be flipped on its head. And Jesus wants them to know: they'll never face the future without his help. Nor will you. You have a travel companion.

When you place your faith in Christ, Christ places his Spirit before, behind, and within you. Not a strange spirit, but the same Spirit: the *parakletos*. Everything Jesus did for his followers, his Spirit does for you. Jesus taught; the Spirit teaches. Jesus healed; the Spirit heals. Jesus comforted; his Spirit comforts. As Jesus sends you into new seasons, he sends his Counselor to go with you.

Are you on the eve of change? Do you find yourself looking into a new chapter? Is the foliage of your world showing signs of a new season? Heaven's message for you is clear: when everything else changes, God's presence never does. You journey in the company of the Holy Spirit, who "will teach you everything and will remind you of everything I have told you" (John 14:26 NLT).

So make friends with whatever's next. Embrace it. Accept it. Don't resist it. Change is not only a part of life;

change is a necessary part of God's strategy. To use us to change the world, he alters our assignments. Gideon: from farmer to general; Mary: from peasant girl to the mother of Christ; Paul: from local rabbi to world evangelist. God transitioned Joseph from a baby brother to an Egyptian prince. He changed David from a shepherd to a king. Peter wanted to fish the Sea of Galilee. God called him to lead the first church. God makes reassignments.

What could he be reassigning you to? Whatever it is, we all have one ultimate assignment in common, one that makes the changes and transitions of this life fade into the background: eternal glory. I'd like a large cup, please. "One venti-sized serving of endless joy in the presence of God. Go heavy on the wonder, and cut all the heartache." Go ahead and request it. The Barista is still brewing. For all you know, it could be the next cup you drink.

Reflection

Spend some time reflecting on what you have read by journaling your thoughts and answers to the following prompts and questions.

1. Is there a change or transition you are facing in your life? How do you feel about this change?

_____

_____

_____

_____

_____

_____

_____

In the past, how have you responded to seasons of change? Has this response been helpful or hurtful? Why?

_____

_____

_____

_____

2. As someone who knows the end of the story, how would you have helped the disciples understand Jesus' announcement that he would be leaving them?

_____

_____

_____

_____

_____

Now, pretend you know the end of your story in the midst of whatever change or transition you are facing. Trust that it will be a hard but good and necessary change. What words of comfort could you give yourself today in the same way you wrote words of comfort to the disciples?

_____

_____

_____

_____

3. What role does the Holy Spirit play in our lives?

_____

_____

_____

_____

How could you rely on the Holy Spirit to help you during this time of change?

_____

_____

_____

_____

4. Have you ever received a "reassignment" from God due to a transition? What was it, and how did it change you?

_____

_____

_____

_____

_____

What reassignment could be in store for you during the
transition you're in now, and how do you feel about it?

_____

_____

_____

_____

_____

_____

God's Word for You

Allow these passages from God's Word to remind you that
God will help you if you need guidance.

> I will love You, O LORD, my strength.
> The LORD is my rock and my fortress and my deliverer;

My God, my strength, in whom I will trust;
My shield and the horn of my salvation, my stronghold.

PSALM 18:1–2

No matter what is changing in your life, God remains the same. He is your rock and stronghold.

For everything there is a season,
a time for every activity under heaven.
A time to be born and a time to die.
A time to plant and a time to harvest.

ECCLESIASTES 3:1–2 NLT

Change comes in seasons, and no season lasts forever.

"I am telling you these things now while I am still with you. But when the Father sends the Advocate as my representative—that is, the Holy Spirit—he will teach you everything and will remind you of everything I have told you. I am leaving you with a gift—peace of mind and heart. And the peace I give is a gift the world cannot give."

JOHN 14:25–27 NLT

The Holy Spirit is a gift who pours peace into your spirit in a way that the world never could.

Read the following prayer, silently or aloud. When you have finished praying, spend a moment in silence, listening for the voice of God.

Dear God, I am not sure what's next in my life, and this makes me feel anxious and afraid. Times of change are hard for me even though they can be exciting. I pray for the presence of your Spirit to be with me and that you would help me to be aware of his presence in my everyday life. Teach me how to rely on the Spirit, talk to the Spirit, and more intimately know the Spirit—this gift that Christ gave us when he left the earth. I am thankful to you that

I don't have to go through this alone, that I have a helper and a teacher. Give me a teachable heart. Make me ready to listen and receive your wisdom, so I am prepared for whatever comes next. In Jesus' name I pray, amen.

CHAPTER 10

God Will Help
You Forgive

Some people abandon the path of forgiveness because they perceive it to be impossibly steep. So let's be realistic about the act. Forgiveness does not pardon the offense, excuse the misdeed, or ignore it. Forgiveness is not necessarily reconciliation. A reestablished relationship with the transgressor is not essential or always even possible. Even more, the phrase "forgive and forget" sets an unreachable standard. Painful memories are not like old clothing. They defy easy shedding.

> A step in the direction of forgiveness is a decisive step toward happiness.

Forgiveness is simply the act of changing your attitude toward the offender; it's moving from a desire to harm toward an openness to be at peace. A step in the direction of forgiveness is a decisive step toward happiness.

When researchers from Duke University listed eight factors that promote emotional stability, four of them related to forgiveness.

1. Avoiding suspicion and resentment.
2. Not living in the past.
3. Not wasting time and energy fighting conditions that can't be changed.
4. Refusing to indulge in self-pity when handed a raw deal.[1]

It's no wonder then that the flotilla of "one another" scriptures listed in Paul's letter to the Ephesians includes one named the USS *Forgiveness*. "Be kind to one another, tenderhearted, forgiving one another, even as God in Christ forgave you" (Ephesians 4:32).

It was not enough for Paul to say, "Forgive one another as your conscience dictates." Or "to the degree that you feel comfortable." Or "as much as makes common sense." No, Paul did what he loved to do: he used Jesus as our standard. Forgive others as Christ forgave you.

So we leave the Epistles and thumb our way leftward into the Gospels, looking for a time in which Jesus forgave others. We are barely through the back entrance to John's gospel before we find an example. The story includes a basin of water, a towel, two dozen sweaty feet, and one dozen disciples.

> Jesus, knowing that the Father had given all things into His hands, and that He had come from God and was going to God, rose from supper and laid aside His garments, took a towel and girded Himself. After that, He poured water into a basin and began to wash the disciples' feet, and to wipe them with the towel with which He was girded. (John 13:3–5)

How much time do you think this cleansing required? Supposing Jesus took two or three minutes per foot, this act would have taken the better part of an hour. Keep in mind, Jesus was down to his final minutes with his followers. If his three years with them were measured by sand in an hourglass, only a few grains had yet to fall. Jesus chose to use them in this silent sacrament of humility.

> If his three years with them were measured by sand in an hourglass, only a few grains had yet to fall.

Later that night the disciples realized the enormity of this gesture. They had pledged to stay with their Master, but those pledges melted like wax in the heat of the Roman torches. When the soldiers marched in, the disciples ran out.

I envision them sprinting until, depleted of strength, they plopped to the ground and let their heads fall forward as they looked wearily at the dirt. That's when they saw the feet Jesus had just washed. That's when they realized he had given them grace before they even knew they needed it.

Jesus forgave his betrayers before they betrayed him.

Hasn't he done the same for us? We've been wounded, perhaps deeply. But haven't we been forgiven preemptively? Before we knew we needed grace, we were offered it.

Suppose I were somehow to come into possession of your sin-history video. Every contrary act. Every wayward thought. Every reckless word. Would you want me to play it on a screen? By no means. You'd beg me not to. And I would beg you not to show mine.

Don't worry. I don't have it. But Jesus does. He's seen it. He's seen every backstreet, back-seat, backhanded moment of our lives. And he has resolved, "My grace is enough. I can cleanse these people. I will wash away their betrayals." For that reason we must make the Upper Room of Mercy our home address.

The apostle John championed this thought of Christ's perpetual cleansing:

> But if we live in the light, as God is in the light, we can share fellowship with each other. Then the blood of Jesus, God's Son, cleanses us from every sin. (1 John 1:7 NCV)

He can be depended on to forgive us and to cleanse us from every wrong. (1 John 1:9 TLB)

Christ, our cleanser. He knew our promises would fall like broken glass. He knew we would dart into a dark alley of shame. He knew we would bury our faces between our knees.

It is in this context that Paul urged us to follow Jesus' lead. To give grace rather than get retribution. To give grace, not because others deserve it but because we've been doused with it. "Forgiving one another, even as God in Christ forgave you" (Ephesians 4:32).

> Wearing the towel and holding the basin, he said to his church, "This is how we do it."

Wearing the towel and holding the basin, he said to his church, "This is how we do it."

"If I then, your Lord and Teacher, have washed your feet, you also ought to wash one another's feet. For I have given you an example, that you should do as I have done to you" (John 13:14–15).

Let others bicker and fight; we don't.

Let others seek revenge; we don't.

Let others keep a list of offenders; we don't.

We take the towel. We fill the basin. We wash one another's feet.

Jesus could do this because he knew who he was—sent from and destined for heaven. And you? Do you know who you are? You are the creation of a good God, made in his image. You are destined to reign in an eternal kingdom. You are only heartbeats away from heaven.

Secure in who you are, you can do what Jesus did. Throw aside the robe of rights and expectations and make the most courageous of moves. Wash feet.

Let's be "tenderhearted, forgiving one another" (Ephesians 4:32).

Tenderhearted: malleable, soft, kind, responsive.

Hard-hearted: cold, stony, unbending.

Which words describe your heart?

To be clear, my aim is not to dismiss a perpetrator or downplay your pain. The question is not, Did you get hurt? The question is, Are you going to let the hurt harden you? Numb you? Suck up all your joy?

Wouldn't you prefer to be "tenderhearted, forgiving one another"?

Try these steps.

Decide what you need to forgive. Get specific. Narrow it down to the identifiable offense. "He was a jerk" does not work. "He promised to leave his work at work and be attentive at home." There, that's better.

Ask yourself why it hurts. Why does this offense sting? What about it leaves you wounded? Do you feel betrayed? Ignored? Isolated? Do your best to find the answer, and before you take it out on the offender . . .

Take it to Jesus. No one will ever love you more than he does. Let this wound be an opportunity to draw near to your Savior. Does this experience and lack of forgiveness hamper your well-being? Does it diminish your peace? If the answer is yes, take steps in the direction of forgiveness. Talk to Jesus about the offense until the anger subsides. And when it returns, talk to Jesus again.

And *if it feels safe,* at some point . . .

Tell your offender. With a clear head and pure motives, file a complaint. Be specific. Not overly dramatic. Simply explain the offense and the way it makes you feel. It might sound something like this: "We agreed to make our home a haven. Yet after dinner you seem to get lost in emails and projects. Consequently, I feel lonely under my own roof."

If done respectfully and honestly, this is a step toward forgiveness. There is nothing easy about broaching a sensitive topic. You are putting on a servant's garb. By bringing it up you are giving forgiveness a chance to have its way and win the day.

Will it? Will grace triumph? There is no guarantee. Whether it does or not, your next step is to . . .

Pray for your offender.

> There is nothing easy about broaching a sensitive topic. You are putting on a servant's garb.

You cannot force reconciliation, but you can offer intercession. "Pray for those who persecute you" (Matthew 5:44 NIV). Prayer reveals any lingering grudge, and what better place to see it! Are you standing before the throne of grace yet finding it difficult to give grace? Ask Jesus to help you.

Here is one final idea:

Conduct a funeral. Bury the offense. I don't mean to bury it in the sense of suppressing it. Nothing is gained by shoving negative emotions into your spirit. But something wonderful is gained by taking the memory, placing it in a casket (a shoebox will suffice), and burying it in the cemetery known as "Moving On with Life." Take off your hat, cover your heart, and shed one final tear. When the anger surfaces again, just tell yourself, "It's time to walk boldly into a bright future."

Are you ready for one of these steps? Perhaps just the first one? If a grudge is holding your spirit, it could be time for you to follow the example of Jesus in the upper room. It could be time to forgive as Christ forgave you.

Reflection

Spend some time reflecting on what you have read by journaling your thoughts and answers to the following prompts and questions.

1. Forgiveness is a tough topic and can raise difficult memories. What thoughts and memories came to mind as you read through today's reading?

_____

_____

_____

_____

_____

_____

_____

Did you think of anyone specific who you need to forgive? If so, who? Why do you need to forgive this person?

_____

_____

_____

_____

2. Read about Jesus' washing the disciples' feet again in John 13:3–5. What stands out to you in the passage?

_____

_____

_____

_____

_____

How would it have felt to be a disciple in the upper room that night?

_____

_____

_____

_____

3. What do you believe the purpose of forgiveness is, and how have you come to that belief? Through personal experience, Scripture, what someone told you? Explain your answer below.

_____

_____

_____

_____

_____

4. Of the steps to forgiveness described in today's reading, which one could you take today in regard to someone you need to forgive? What would taking that step look like for you?

_____

_____

_____

_____

God's Word for You

Allow these passages from God's Word to remind you that God will help you forgive.

> You, Lord, are forgiving and good,
> abounding in love to all who call to you.
>
> PSALM 86:5 NIV

God does not reserve a little love and forgiveness for each of us. He has plenty and gives generously to all who come to him.

Then Peter came to Him and said, "Lord, how often shall my brother sin against me, and I forgive him? Up to seven times?"

Jesus said to him, "I do not say to you, up to seven times, but up to seventy times seven."

MATTHEW 18:21–22

Forgiveness is not a one-time act; it is a posture we hold toward others.

And be kind to one another, tenderhearted, forgiving one another, even as God in Christ forgave you.

EPHESIANS 4:32

We forgive because he first forgave us.

Read the following prayer, silently or aloud. When you have finished praying, spend a moment in silence, listening for the voice of God.

Dear God, I confess that forgiveness does not come naturally to me. I can hold on to a grudge for too long. I remember how people have hurt me. I remember who has hurt me. And I'm afraid if I forgive them, they will get off too easy. I want to take justice into my own hands. But I know Jesus provides another way—one of grace, love, and peace—in which I am not responsible for judging someone and can let go of past offenses. Soften my heart toward Jesus' way. Show me how to forgive in the way I have been forgiven. Thank you for sending your Son, so that I can always know I am forgiven for my sin. As I grow more aware of the way you've forgiven me, may I extend forgiveness to others. In Jesus' name, amen.

Conclusion

Andres Lopez thought he could ride out the hurricane in his fishing boat. Irma was bearing down on the Florida Coast. Advisories were warning residents to batten down and boaters to seek safety. The storm had already created havoc in the Caribbean and threatened to do the same to Miami.

Lopez heard the warnings and knew the dangers; still, he believed he and his twenty-five-foot fishing boat could survive. He was only half right. As the waves began to roar, his craft began to bounce. His cabin spun like the interior of a washing machine. Water poured in and he was thrown from side to side.

He did not want to abandon ship. His beloved *Run Running* was more than a recreational vessel, it was his home. Lopez wasn't a polished member of the yacht society; he was the equivalent of a sea squatter, a live-aboard sailor who anchored off the coast of Coconut Grove. He made his living selling fish and cleaning boat bottoms. His fifty-six years have left their mark; he's lost most of his hearing and most of his teeth. And he wasn't about to lose his boat.

He hunkered down hoping to hold on. But the sky turned black and lightning began to pop. His boat listed starboard at an extreme angle. He climbed up on deck, surveyed his options, and made his decision. He dove into Biscayne Bay and began swimming. He looked back in time to see his boat flip over. He flailed his way through one hundred yards of white-capped waves. He crawled onto a sliver of sand that serves as a wind break. He had just enough time to spit out saltwater and catch his breath before a storm surge lifted him another two hundred *yards*, dumping him against a baseball field backstop in a city park.

Rescuers found him scraped, scratched, and soaked to the bone. But he was alive. "You've seen that movie, *The Perfect Storm*," he said. "This was my disaster movie."

Don't we all have one? At some point in life, the hurricane hits, the heavenly valve opens, our vessel bounces like a Ping-Pong ball in a wind tunnel, and we wonder, we really wonder, if we are going to drown.

Perhaps you are feeling the storm today. The storm of isolation? Trepidation? The waves roar. The thunder claps. And your heart pounds.

The most famous of storm stories involves not a fishing boat near Miami but a fishing boat in Galilee. The disciples had spent the night rowing through the towering waves. Soaked to the skin from the rain, voices hoarse from the shouting, they saw a figure drawing near. "They saw Jesus approaching the boat, walking on the water" (John 6:19 NIV).

Of all the places to see Jesus, they saw him in the storm.

My prayer is that you will do the same.

When skies of relationship turn dark. When winds of worry rock your world. When waves of pain overwhelm you. See him. Hear his voice. The One who cares. The same God who walked on water is your ever-present help.

"Don't be afraid, I've redeemed you. I've called your name. You're mine.

When you're in over your head, I'll be there with you.

When you're in rough waters, you will not go down. . . .

I am GOD, your personal God, The Holy of Israel, your Savior. . . .

So don't be afraid: I'm with you." (Isaiah 43:1–5 MSG)

Is your world stormy? No one disputes the struggles of life. As sure as the storm is the promise of God to calm it. When you cannot find him, he will find you.

Then they cry out to the LORD in their trouble, And He brings them out of their distresses. He calms the storm, So that its waves are still. (Psalm 107:28–29).

God will help you.

Notes

Introduction

1. Patrick Henry Hughes, *I Am Potential* (Lifelong Publishing, 2008), 3.
2. Rick Reilly, "Trumpeting the Father of the Year," *Sports Illustrated*, October 16, 2006, https://vault.si.com/vault /2006/10/16/trumpeting-the-father-of-the-year .

Chapter 1: God Will Help You When You Feel Anxious

1. Edmund J. Bourne, *The Anxiety and Phobia Workbook*, 5th ed. (Oakland, CA: New Harbinger, 2010), xi.
2. Taylor Clark, "It's Not the Job Market: The Three Real Reasons Why Americans Are More Anxious than Ever Before," *Slate*, January 31, 2011, http://www.slate.com /articles/arts/culturebox/2011/01/its_not_the_job_market .html.
3. John Ortberg, *Soul Keeping: Caring for the Most Important Part of You* (Grand Rapids, MI: Zondervan, 2014), 46.
4. Clark, "It's Not the Job Market."
5. Clark, "It's Not the Job Market."

6. Robert L. Leahy, *Anxiety Free: Unravel Your Fears Before They Unravel You* (Carlsbad, CA: Hay House, 2009), 4.
7. Bourne, *The Anxiety and Phobia Workbook*, xi.
8. Joel J. Miller, "The Secret Behind the Bible's Most Highlighted Verse," *Patheos*, June 6, 2013, https://www.patheos.com/blogs/joeljmiller/2013/06/the-secret-behind-the-bibles-most-highlighted-verse/.

Chapter 2: God Will Help You Solve Your Problems

1. Translation by Frederick Dale Bruner, *The Gospel of John: A Commentary* (Grand Rapids, MI: Eerdmans, 2012), 359.
2. Bruner, *Gospel of John*, 359.
3. Bruner, *Gospel of John*, 359.
4. Exodus 2:6; Genesis 41:9–14; 1 Samuel 17:48–49; Matthew 27:32–54.

Chapter 3: God Will Help You Through Your Fears

1. Shelley Wachsmann, *The Sea of Galilee Boat: An Extraordinary 2000 Year Old Discovery* (New York: Plenum Press, 1995), 39, 121.

Chapter 4: God Will Help You When You Feel Stuck

1. More recent translations of this passage have chosen to remove a curious reference to an angel who would, on

occasion, stir the surface. The first person to touch the water after the bubbles appeared would be healed. Almost all evangelical scholars agree that these words were added by a redactor or editor who wanted to explain why people came to the pool. Whether the phrase was a part of John's original text or not, the fact remains that the pool of Bethesda was encircled by crowds of sick people—"Blind, lame, or paralyzed [that] lay on the porches" (v. 3).

2. "Bethesda," BibleWalks.com, https://biblewalks.com/Sites /Bethesda.html.

Chapter 6: God Will Help You in Your Everyday Life

1. Six water jars of 25 gallons each equals 150 gallons. There are 128 ounces in a gallon, so 150 gallons would equal 19,200 ounces. A wine bottle typically holds 25.4 ounces, so 19,200 ounces would fill 756 bottles.

Chapter 8: God Will Help You Get Through Grief

1. Bruner, *Gospel of John*, 664.

Chapter 10: God Will Help You Forgive

1. "Peace of Mind," a sociological study conducted by Duke University, cited in Rudy A. Magnan, *Reinventing American Education: Applying Innovative and Quality*

Thinking to Solving Problems in Education (Bloomington, IN: Xlibris, 2010), 23. These are the other four: (1) Staying involved with the living world. (2) Cultivating old-fashioned virtues: love, humor, compassion, and loyalty. (3) Not expecting too much of oneself. (4) Finding something bigger than oneself to believe in.

About the
Author

Since entering the ministry in 1978, Max Lucado has served churches in Miami, Florida; Rio de Janeiro, Brazil; and San Antonio, Texas. He currently serves as Teaching Minister of Oak Hills Church in San Antonio. He is America's bestselling inspirational author with more than 140 million books in print.

Visit his website at MaxLucado.com
Facebook.com/MaxLucado
Instagram.com/MaxLucado
Twitter.com/MaxLucado

Grace for the Moment© has touched millions of lives with inspirational thoughts for every day that emphasize the help and hope of God in everyday moments. This large deluxe edition offers a leather-flex cover, beautifully designed pages with large type, and a ribbon marker.

- Each devotion encourages readers to grow their faith by embracing the hope of the Lord every day.
- Each daily reading features devotional writings from Max's numerous bestsellers as well as a Scripture verse selected especially for each day's reading.
- The *Grace for the Moment©* large deluxe edition is perfect for any occasion.

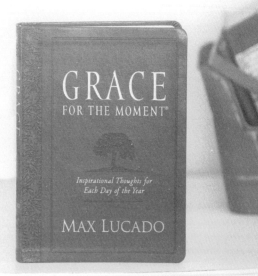